An Occultist's Travels
by Willy Reichel

An Occultist's Travels

by
Willy Reichel

Running Press
Philadelphia, Pennsylvania

Copyright © 1975 Running Press
All Rights Reserved Under the Pan-American and
International Copyright Convention

Printed in The United States of America

Distributed in Canada by Van Nostrand Reinhold
Ltd., Ontario

Library of Congress Catalog Card Number 74-31539

ISBN 0-914294-10-5

This book may not be marketed nor sold in France
or French territories

Concept and research by Richard Nicholls

Cover design by Jim Wilson

This book may be ordered directly from the
publisher. Please include 25¢ postage.
Try your bookstore first.

Running Press, 38 South 19th Street,
Philadelphia, Pennsylvania 19103

Colin Wilson:
Notes on An Occultist's Travels

This book is a record of one of the strangest epochs in the history of the human spirit. It is also a fragment of an immense, unsolved mystery story.

That mystery story began on March 31, 1848, when loud rapping noises echoed through the house of the Fox family in Arcadia, New York. Mrs. Fox, understandably upset, invited neighbors in to hear the strange noises, which only occured when her two daughters, ages twelve and fifteen, were present. It was assumed that this was a straightforward case of haunting, and the basement was actually dug up in search for the bones of a peddler who was supposed to have been murdered there. Searchers *did* in fact find a decomposed body, but the odd thing is that the rapping noises continued to follow the Fox sisters around. That certainly eliminated the haunting theory.

Undoubtedly, all this amounted to what we would now call the poltergeist phenomenon. The Fox case created an absolute sensation; people all over America found that they also could "communicate" with "spirits" by means of rapping noises. Then two brothers named Davenport discovered that there was an even more interesting method of contacting the spirits. They would go into a trance, and spirits would take up musical instruments and play them in the dark. These trance subjects soon became known as "mediums," and the spirits of the dead not only came and spoke through their mouths, but also manifested themselves in other ways —even materializing in the room and holding discussions with their still-living relatives!

What we must grasp is that until the mid-19th century, such things were virtually unknown. Certainly there had been plenty of ghosts and poltergeists ever since Roman times. For example, in the time of the first Queen Elizabeth, the alchemist Dr. John Dee had hired a series of young men gifted with "psychic powers" —such as second-sight, telepathy, etc. Dee called these young men "scryers" (meaning "descryers," or see-ers). The most notable scryer was an Irish ex-criminal named Edward Kelly, who gazed into a crystal ball, went into a trance, and held long conversations with "spirits" whom Dee believed to be angels. Kelley's spirits were almost certainly the same kind of spirits that the Davenport brothers contacted almost three centuries later; Kelley was a "medium" —but no one knew it. In the mid-18th century, a retired Swedish engineer named Emanuel Swedenborg found that he had an ability to go into a trance, during which he apparently visited heaven and hell. What Swedenborg, Kelley, and many others had in common was that despite their mediumistic abilities, they apparently were unable to convey spirit messages through their mouths.

All this changed almost overnight in the mid-19th century, an era which we could safely call a "psychic explosion." Spiritualist writers announced portentously that a new age had dawned, as world-shaking as Christianity. According to them, God had chosen Jesus Christ as his messenger to the human race, but now (or so it seemed) He had decided to try direct communication, permitting spirits of the dead to return to earth. All this had an absolutely staggering impact upon our great-great grandparents, to a degree that we can today scarcely imagine. Perhaps we can get *some* idea if we imagine a saucer-like spacecraft landing at the United Nations Plaza in New York City, piloted by little green men announcing that they have traveled from the Andromeda constellation.

We can get an idea about turn-of-the-century spiritualism from this remarkable book by Willy Reichel, a German professor of "mesmerism" with considerable healing powers. *An Occultist's Travels* describes, quite simply, Reichel's travels from New York to Japan in the early years of the present century, and the things he saw and heard: America was, at that time, apparently bursting with gifted mediums and fortune tellers, and Reichel's account leads one to believe that many of them were genuine. (He claims that one palmist had foretold the 1906 San Francisco earthquake in an article published by a local newspaper well in advance of the disaster, which should be easy enough to verify.)

In Chapter Three, you will find a statement that puts the finger on the central problem of all this spiritualistic activity. Reichel comments on the information that "spirits" have given the living about life after death, adding a warning that, in spite of the convincing nature of so many communications, "the relative value of these statements . . . is to be accepted very critically, since, according to experience, they contradict themselves with different mediums. . ." In other words, spirit messages were far from infallible. Because it all tended to be confused and self-contradictory, one might speculate that if there really *were* spirits, they might have been deliberately giving skeptics an excuse for dismissing the whole spirit phenomena as hysteria.

This raises another interesting point. That period was then the era when hysteria was the commonest emotional disorder. Hysteria has almost disappeared today, having been replaced by other mental illnesses. Significantly, "spiritualist" activity has also diminished. Modern spiritualists themselves admit that the age of "great" mediums seems to be over.

Why? What precisely happened? Read this book, and ask yourself those questions. If all Reichel says is true, then spiritualism is *very* important. It should have forced science to completely reverse its foundations. Instead, for the most part, scientists sat tight and insisted that the occult explosion was all a lot of nonsense and would soon blow over. And history proved them more right than wrong.

I have no tidy explanation to offer . . . except the obvious one. While I am not a dedicated spiritualist, I am inclined to accept the notion of some sort of "life after death" rather than not. But I also suspect that what man *really* discovered in the mid-19th century were the strange forces produced by his own subconscious —or *super*conscious— mind. Before we can even begin to grasp what happened, we may need a completely new picture of nature. We may have to accept, for example, that just as there is a "luminiferous ether" that conducts electromagnetic vibrations, so there is another kind of ether that conducts *mental* vibrations.

If Cleve Backster's experiments are correct when they indicate that plants can sense our thoughts, then perhaps we are *all* in contact through this mysterious jelly-like medium, although man's highly developed conscious intellect apparently cuts him off from most of the "vibrations." Cats can see in the dark; perhaps plants can "see" in this psychic darkness, in which the rest of us are blind. But the unconscious —or superconscious— mind may be in contact with this darkness, and can produce effects on it; hence poltergeist activities, telepathy, second-sight and the rest.

Twenty years ago, a majority of readers would have dismissed Willy Reichel's book as a collection of inexplicable absurdities. Now, I think, we are at last ready to take it seriously.

Colin Wilson
Gorran Haven
Cornwall
England
November, 1974

PREFACE.

The first portion of the present work has already appeared in Paris under the title of "A Travers le Monde" (Frédéric Gittler, publisher), and in Germany under that of "Kreuz und Quer durch die Welt" (Leipzig, Oswald Mutze), also in abridged form in England, as "Occult Experiences" (London, Office of *Light*).

The second portion is new, and I hope that the book will meet with as favourable a reception in the United States, where I have lived for the last five years, as has been the case in the above-mentioned countries.

I am a devotee of experimental occultism as understood by Professor Zöllner of Leipzig, the late Dr. du Prel of Munich, and Baron Hellenbach of Vienna, and I hold the view that in our age Natural Science can only be convinced as to the existence of a Future Life by experiment.

I am well aware that Theosophy is familiar

PREFACE

with the phenomena of Spiritualism, and acknowledges them and expects them to exist, but Theosophy has to do only with ethics, philosophy, and its own practical development; and I hold that as yet we have not arrived at this stage of advancement.

The academic science of to-day still disputes the basis, the very existence of these phenomena, but every little contribution adds to the great structure of Truth.

WILLY REICHEL.
Hamilton, Bermuda Islands, July, 1908.

An Occultist's Travels.

I.

After the strain upon my nerves in the year 1900, caused by the previous brutal persecutions on the part of certain representatives of the medical world in Germany, together with the opposition of the clergy, as an expounder of animal magnetism and occult and spiritualistic science, had reached a degree which compelled relaxation, I set out on my travels in order to forget these troubles and to continue my studies. I have traversed France, England, Italy, Africa, America from the Atlantic to the Pacific, Japan, China, the Philippines and Hawaiian Islands, and will now undertake to sketch briefly the new impressions received by me during these extensive journeys, in doing which I assume that the kind reader will take some interest in my personal experiences, especially those in the occult sphere.

I am fifty years old, and there are probably not many men who, from their earliest youth, have travelled so extensively. Experts in chiromancy (or palmistry, as the science is called in England and America) have told me that the lines of my hand showed a predestination for long journeys, especially the well-known chiromancer, Mme. de Thèbes in Paris, whom I visited twice. By the time I was twenty I had travelled through the Riviera, Italy, Austria, Hungary, and Russia. And I have pleasant memories of the time when, in the ruins of Pompeii, I read Bulwer's exciting romances, "The Last Days of Pompeii," and "Zanoni," which latter work ought not to remain unknown to any adherent of transcendental beliefs.

Since then I have passed through fourteen years of conflict, especially the last ten, during which I struggled hard for the recognition of animal magnetism.*

But, during this time, I often visited my

---

*See my book, *Healing Magnetism, Its Relations to Somnambulism and Hypnotism* (Berlin, K. Siegismund), 1896, 3d edition.

favourite spot, Monte Carlo, on the Riviera, which I could do without injury, as I never gamble. To any one who leads a life in which mentality predominates, this jewel of nature is a spot whose beauty materially lightens for him the conditions of intensifying the action of the mind. Often and often have I sat on a bench, high up on the cliffs of Monaco, olive, orange, and lemon trees seeming to smile at me, when I fixed my thoughts upon the mysterious organization of human nature. So I visited Monte Carlo, and again feelings which I believed long buried awoke within me. I then sought various mediums in Nice and Paris, without, however, experiencing anything that could interest wider circles.

In January of the year 1902, which brought me many psychical storms, I set out for Egypt, boarding at Trieste the Austrian Lloyd steamer "Semiramis," on which I reached Alexandria in four days. A storm off the Ionian Islands and while passing Crete, had refreshed my wearied spirit, for I love the elements of nature and am entirely free from seasickness; but unfortunately Poseidon did not let my servant, with whom I shared my cabin, go free.

From Alexandria I went to Cairo (Grand Continental Hotel), Luxor, Thebes, Assouan, and the island of Philæ, which belongs to Nubia. At Elephantine, an island in the Nile opposite Assouan, a desert sand storm surprised me, for one does not walk unmolested beneath palm trees. I stood with reverence in ancient Thebes—now a heap of ruins covered with the sand of the desert—before the tombs of Ramses and the Colossus of Memnon; and the gigantic foundations of the temples in Karnak again showed me how everything in this world, even though it seems built for eternity, must submit to the lot of transitoriness.*

What I experienced in "Babylon," Cairo, and the pyramids of Ghizeh, does not belong here. The East is so utterly unlike the West, and my spirit so sorely needed the change! But the rides through the desert, though often very fatiguing at a temperature of 110 degrees in February, relieved me from rheumatism, which I had brought with me from Europe. Besides,

---

*In the vast cemetery of Sakkara, near ancient Memphis, besides the tombs of Ti and Mera, I regretted that I did not have with me a good trance or speech medium, which regret continued as I sailed up and down the sacred Nile, and passed those ancient abodes of civilization, Denderah, Edfu, Komombo and Esneh.

on this journey I made a dear friend, an Austrian counsel and doctor of jurisprudence. He was my constant companion, and we became deeply attached to each other; it is so seldom that we meet any one with whom we really agree.

In March, at Port Said, I went on board the North German Lloyd steamer "Prussia," which was coming from China, and in five days it carried me past Crete, Sicily, Capri, and Naples to Genoa. In Genoa, news awaited me which summoned me to London. From tropical heat I now crossed the snow ridges of Mont Cenis to Paris, and then went over the Channel to Dover and London. I visited there mediums recommended to me by *Light,* but again without any result worth mentioning. In May and June I was here and there in Germany, until at last the time had come which I had long anticipated, when I was to leave Europe for a long period and visit the New World. Circumstances of no farther interest were now in so satisfactory a form, that I resolved to set out on the voyage across the ocean. On the 10th of July, 1902, I boarded at Cuxhaven the "Prince Bismarck" of the Hamburg-Amerika line, and on the 18th of July arrived safely in New York. I had previously visited many harbours: Genoa, Trieste, Marseilles, Naples, Brindisi, Alexandria, Port Said, Dover, Calais, Cherbourg, Kiel, Cronstadt, St. Petersburg, etc., but not one of them compares in magnificence with the harbour of New York. The first sight of it is simply overwhelming! Mr. Hermann Handrich, of the Swiss Consulate, most pleasantly known as a contributor to German psychical reviews, as well as by his hospitality, received me cordially, and took me to a medium whose specialty is direct writing on a tablet. I am positive that this is a genuine medium, especially as Mr. Handrich, one of the best practical experts, was himself present, but the purport of the writing received did not impress me. I did not expect anything remarkable, since I have found by experience that it is very rare to obtain much at a first seance, even with the best mediums. To do so certainly requires patience.

When I reached New York in July, most of the mediums were in the country, and so Mr. Handrich advised me to visit the Spiritualist "Camp" at Lily Dale. I left New York on the night train, passed through Poughkeepsie (where the seer, Andrew Jackson Davis, was born) in the handsome, well arranged Pullman car, then went on to Niagara Falls, and the next noon reached Dunkirk on Lake Erie, from which a small branch road goes to Lily Dale. Violent rains had washed away the embankment of the road, so after waiting nearly six hours at the little station, I determined to take a carriage, in order at least to reach Lily Dale by night.

The liberty of Spiritualism here is entirely different from what it is in Europe! Charmingly situated on Cassadaga Lake, N. Y., the little wooden houses of the mediums stretch in various directions; perhaps fifty of all descriptions live here together. Before each house is a sign, stating the kind of power the occupant possesses, and no one disturbs them in the exercise of their calling; on the contrary strangers come here from all quarters, seeking the mediums which seem to them best suited to their purpose. I can say that I was most kindly received, perhaps partly because my name was not unknown there, as I have contributed a great deal for several years to American publications. So I visited many trance, speech, and materialization mediums. True, I did not obtain much here, at least concerning the question of identity, which perhaps can never be proved, aside from the fact that it is probably extremely difficult for foreign intelligencies, that is, in this case the Germans who were closely connected with me, to put themselves, quickly and without ceremony, into communication with American mediums, whose views and comprehension of life are in many respects wholly different from theirs.

I have seen at the séances of the mediums Winans and A. Normann, within two hours, in the presence of perhaps thirty people, probably twelve different materialized phantoms, large and small, Indians, Englishmen, and Americans, each of whom appealed to some one present to prove himself a relative or friend. I, too, was summoned, but I could not recognize the being in question as the person he alleged himself to be. I will enter no farther into details, as I am writing no scientific treatise, but merely a brief account of travel. I also made the acquaintance in Lily Dale of Mr. Bach, the estimable editor of the *Sunflower,* then published there, who advised me very strongly to visit the Bangs Sisters in Chicago (654 West Adams street) which I did, and did not regret it.

Miss Bangs possesses a very peculiar power as a medium, which I had never witnessed before. A letter is written to some intelligence from whom one desires to receive a communication, a few empty sheets are enclosed for a reply, then the envelope is sealed with one's own seal and put between two slates on a table in the bright sunshine. Miss Bangs, after placing an inkstand and a penholder on the slate, sits down opposite with folded arms. The noise of writing is now distinctly heard, then rapping, and then the slate may be taken. My letter lay exactly as I had left it, with the seal uninjured. I opened it, and all the empty pages were filled with writing in ink, and all this was done at noon, in broad daylight! In spite of all scepticism, I could discover no fraud there, and, besides, Miss Bangs enjoys a very good reputation in initiated circles.

From Chicago I set out on my journey to California, which I dreaded slightly, for travelling four nights and three days uninterruptedly does not suit every one. I took the shortest route, by the "Union Pacific." Nothing but endless prairies—enough to drive one to despair! Through Illinois, Iowa, Nebraska, Wyoming, Nevada—a cheerless wilderness! The mountain chain presents no variety, since in this tract the land rises very gradually until one has reached the Sierra Nevada, whose rocks are grotesque in form. At last the train draws near California, and now vegetation seems entirely changed. I did not remain long in San Francisco, as I wanted to go to Southern California. After a further ride of eighteen hours one reaches Los Angeles. This is the place where Frau Valeska Töpfer, a medium of great renown in Germany, spent the last four years of her life. I arrived there the 1st of August, 1902. It is still a comparatively new city, at the junction of the Southern Pacific and the Santa Fé railroads. On this account its growth has been incredibly rapid, even for American conditions. All kinds of tropical plants—only the dates and bananas do not ripen—grow there in unexpected magnificence, which is increased by countless humming-birds.

Situated at the foot of the Sierra Nevada, three quarters of an hour distant from the ocean, it possesses a climate superior to that of the Riviera, for I could not endure the heat there in April, while in Los Angeles, after noon, there is a sea breeze from the ocean which renders the nights cool.

I should like to tell a great deal about the magnificent natural advantages of Southern California, but I lack the pen of a Ludwig Pietsch. The Americans have treated me with the utmost cordiality, and are generally very courteous and hospitable; I have not a word to say on that score. The country, however, lacks the Art, and especially the poetry, of which the German is so proud. There, too, I sought out various mediums. California is the land of the medium and the "Magnetic Healer;" a Spiritualist camp was just being formed. At a materialization medium's I visited there (Mr. George Brower), I saw probably eight phantoms within an hour who all appeared in white veils, whereas the figures at the Normann's in Lily Dale, previously mentioned, showed themselves in the clothes they wore in life. It is not clear to me why the spirits in Los Angeles appeared in one way and those in Lily Dale in another.

By the advice of many acquaintances I visited, in August, 1903, the famous Yosemite National Park and the Mariposa Big Trees in Northern California. The Yosemite Valley lies about 4000 feet above the sea, and its mountains, Clouds' Rest, for instance, attain a height of 9912 feet. As almost everything is made possible in America, the Southern Pacific railroad has built a little hotel on Glacier Point (7201 feet high), which can be reached only on horseback along sheer precipices and waterfalls. Here I passed the night. Never shall I forget the view from this point over those grotesque peaks. A ride down of about ten hours, in a stage, brings one to the Mariposa Big Tree Grove. These primeval giants are difficult to describe. Whoever has not seen them himself will believe it a fairy tale to hear of trees 405 feet tall and 110 feet in circumference. Professor David Starr Jordan, of Stanford University, believes that some of these trees —they are called Sequoia, a species of pine— are over 8000 years old. The Pyramid of Cheops, which I saw in Egypt in 1902, was built about 2170 B.C. A scholar has made the assertion that these trees had bark a foot thick

An Occultist's Travels. 21

when Cheops' hundred thousand men began their thirty years' labour in building this pyramid.

Having returned to Southern California, various circumstances compelled me, at the end of September, to go to San Francisco. I went by ship, which, leaving the harbour, Port Los Angeles (three-quarters of an hour distant from the city of that name), reaches the capital of California in about twenty-five hours. Whales and flying fish were our constant companions. The publisher of the *Philosophical Journal,* J. Munsell Chase (Dr. Newman, the former editor, died in April), gave me, at my request for the addresses of first-class mediums, the names of Mrs. Wermouth (416 Golden Gate avenue) as an excellent trance medium, and Mr. C. V. Miller (1084 Bush street) as the best materialization medium. Mrs. Wermouth gave good proofs; she told me at once that I possessed an unusually strong and pure magnetic power, in connection with which I will remark that I had not previously mentioned to her either my name or my profession. Mrs. S. Seal (1424 Market street) is also very good as a trance and healing medium.

Mr. Miller must be described more fully, since my experiences with him surpassed everything that I had previously known, at least in his character as a materialization medium.* Mr. Miller then owned a business in Japanese art wares and old pictures at 568 Geary street, and his appearance, with his modest bearing, is very prepossessing. After a long interval he had just begun again to give seances. I mentioned neither my name, nor my occupation, because he did not ask for them. On Thursday, October 1st, 1903, I went to him and found there twenty-five persons, both men and women. His so-called cabinet was a bow-window of three sections, with a curtain of black material, facing directly upon the street. When I entered, the curtain was drawn back, and I investigated everything in the most thorough manner. To come in from the outside was utterly impossible, as Bush street is well frequented and fully lighted by lamps, so that any attempt to enter from without would be im-

---

*See also my article in *La Revue Spirite,* Paris, August, 1904; "Materializations," in *The Harbinger of Light,* Melbourne, October, 1904; also in *Le Messager,* Liége, Dec. 15th, 1904, and in *The Banner of Light,* Boston, Jan. 7th, 1905.

practicable on account of the pedestrians constantly passing. Miller first requested every one present to search this bow-window thoroughly, and he really made so pleasant, simple and frank an impression that harmony, which is a principal matter in such seances, was not difficult to establish. After several persons had changed their places, which is usually necessary at such seances for the proper combination of the fluid emanations of those present, he placed himself *before* the curtain, which directly afterwards was opened, and now phantom after phantom appeared, whom he, without being in a trance, took by the hand and first asked for the name, which was instantly given. After the appearance of the second phantom he said suddenly: "Here is a Spirit, who calls himself So-and-so"—he mentioned a name known to me—"and says that Moppel, a dog that is still alive, remembers you vividly, and is faithfully guarding your home." Now for the explanation. At my temporary home in Southern California, I had a very faithful white Alaska dog, which I had left there, and to which I had given the name of "Moppel." No one in this seance knew me, or was aware that

I was living at that time in Southern California and owned a dog named Moppel. Besides, it is a German dog-name, and Miller does not understand a word of German! The spirit, who said this, was, as I have said, known to me by name and seemed to be very familiar with my private affairs.

After a number of spirits had first mentioned their names, they summoned several of those present and talked with them. Some of those asked for were not present, upon which the spirits withdrew with words of regret. Mr. Miller then stated that he would retire into the cabinet, because then the phantoms have more power, and from it they would go to those present. And so it was! Scarcely four minutes had elapsed, when the curtain opened entirely and Mr. Miller was seen asleep, with six fully developed phantoms in white robes beside him, who all clasped hands. Gradually the different phantoms came out of the cabinet, went to those present, and talked eagerly with them; two spoke German. As I heard later, they were conversing with Germans. Suddenly I heard distinctly, loudly, and clearly a name which I knew very well, from a phantom who wished to

An Occultist's Travels. 25

speak to me. Enough—they are private matters, concerning which I must keep silent. Another phantom came close to me, bowed, and I recognized it; his name, which he then uttered, corresponded. Almost at the same moment that the last phantom withdrew from our circle, Mr. Miller came out of the cabinet. There was ample light during the whole seance. The following phenomenon was also extremely interesting: a white ball, which looked like muslin, hovered a short time *in front of* the curtain, then sank before the eyes of all, and in scarcely two minutes a new spirit figure formed itself.*

The dematerializations principally took place in full view, in front of the curtain. I can only say that during many years I have seen a great deal, but nothing like this, and I only regret that Germany does not possess such a medium. Unfortunately I was obliged to go away, but I hoped at no distant time to see Mr. Miller again.

---

*The same phenomenon, only taking a longer time for development, is described by Mme. d'Espérance in her work, *Shadowland.* See also *Uebersinnliche Welt* (Supernatural World), Berlin, Max Rahn, 1900, p. 67; also Dr. Alfred Russel Wallace, *A Defence of Modern Spiritualism,* and Mary Karadja, *Spiritistische Phaenomene* (Spiritualistic Phenomena), Leipsic, M. Spohr, p. 15, etc.

I subsequently read in the April number of *Psychical Studies,* Leipzig, of 1903 (page 243) a notice of Mr. Miller; Professor Maier correctly points out in a footnote that Miller was not bound at that time, and I am of the same opinion as R. Seithel, Sr. (*Psychical Studies,* 1900, p. 578) that binding is by no means a humane method of control, and phenomena occurring when it is used will be no more uncontrovertible than without it. At this extremely interesting seance I only observed, and immediately wrote down truthfully what I saw and heard; I examined the cabinet thoroughly before and after the seance; I saw Miller almost constantly along with the phantoms, and perceived no sign of apparatus or trickery. Yet Baron Von Hellenbach is right when he says in his *Vorurteile der Menschheit* (Prejudices of Mankind), published by Mutze in Leipzig, III, p. 239: "There is a scepticism, which can even surpass in stupidity the ignorant superstitions of a mountain charcoal-burner."

In December, 1903, I spent some time in San Diego, the last city this side the Mexican frontier; the Coronado Hotel there, built on

Coronado Beach, is probably the most aristocratic place on the coast of Southern California. Near San Diego (a carriage drive of an hour and a half) at Point Loma, the Theosophists have built a wonderful monastery, from which one has a magnificent view of the wide ocean, San Diego Bay, and the Mexican mountains. In winter, after the heat has somewhat diminished, everything grows here in tropical glory of colour. The wonderful bignonias and the superb bougainvilleas with their thousands of yellowish red and blue flowers here twine around almost every one of the little houses, which, of course, on account of the frequent earthquakes, are built of wood, as they are nearly everywhere in California. In this institution Theosophy is taught according to the ideas of Mme. Blavatsky. Point Loma Homestead is the name of the monastery, in which any one who is seeking rest and recuperation can find accommodation at the rate of three dollars a day.

In January, I spent some time in the San Gabriel Cañon, a part of the South Californian Sierra Nevada, and there learned the hard calling of the gold miner. Here the principal methods are the so-called dry digging (digging in sandbanks, hills, mountains) and the cioting digging (from a species of animal "ciot"), found everywhere in this region, which digs in the earth. Strict laws prevail in these mountains. Every thief is pursued and shot without mercy. The gold miner, who lives in a tent, to which every one has easy access, spends the day in his mine, and his tent is usually filled with stores of provisions, which are brought on horses from long distances. Any one can take from them, but he must leave a note there, stating who he is, and what he has carried away, or "to horse,"—the search for him begins, and woe betide him! I spent the winter in these mountains very comfortably, rode to the mines almost daily, often helped in washing the gold, and met among these people very excellent men, who hospitably offered me everything they possessed (dried canned goods and fried bacon). There was only one Indian, whose Spanish-English-Indian dialect was difficult to understand, whose insolence forced me to hold a loaded revolver under his nose; but I had been warned against him. I have often met this race in various parts of the United States and in Mexico, but have almost always found them peaceful.

The rest of the time I spent in trout-fishing and hunting. Here the California bears may still be found, and in summer numerous serpents, especially the dangerous rattlesnake. The temperature in these mountains in January is about the same as it is in May in Germany. My equipment was shoes with spiked soles, a revolver in my pocket, and an iron-shod cane; many days I rode on horseback for six or eight hours through mountain streams and over peaks, and then in the evening, in Follows Camp, where I lived, made a fire in the little iron stove, for at night it grew cold. I had with me a few works by Schopenhauer, Hellenbach, du Prel, as well as several volumes of *"Psychical Studies"* and the *"Transcendental World,"* so that I could also keep my mind employed.

II

From December until the end of March Los Angeles is crowded with invalids and people who wish to escape the cold weather of the eastern states. It is a five days' journey from New York, but one is rewarded as soon as the Rocky Mountains are crossed; for the climate of Southern California in winter is about the same as I found in Sicily, only the magnificent floral display is greater in California. As soon as the first rain begins to fall in December or January, after an interval of nearly seven months, everything commences to grow with wonderful luxuriance. With these strangers a number of mediums usually arrive, and so now came a "Count Gabriel Dizara," who calls himself "Anglo-Hindu Palmist and Medium, Member of the Ancient Order of Occult Scientists, Psychical Research Society of America," and President of the "Balfour Institute of Science"

An Occultist's Travels. 31

in New York. He boasts of knowing the secrets of the Lama priests, and will allow himself to be buried six days, like some Hindu fakirs. At any rate, he is an interesting man. I wrote in my lodgings a number of questions, put them in a closed envelope, and went to him. His companion burned *before my eyes* this closed envelope in a second room before I had seen Mr. Dizara at all, with the remark that these questions would now be considered and answered by the "Professor," without my having said a word. Directly after I was called into another room, and stood opposite to this man, who clasped my left hand and repeated all my questions successively, with accurate pronunciation of proper names, at the same time answering them. Whether his statements will prove correct, the future must determine. I can certify that no one had read my questions, and that they were previously burned in their original condition before my eyes in another room. I am outlining all that I experienced very briefly, in order not to bring upon myself the reproach of prolixity; but after my experiences in America, I shall regard with different eyes the much-assailed book by Florence Marryat, *"There is no Death."* Until that time, I, too, thought this lady somewhat fantastic. But Hellenbach is evidently right in saying: "The unbelieving world, taught and elucidated in its imagination, wants no heaven at all; it would feel the full measure of its absurdity if the intelligible world would take a firm stand and admit the great error of opinion it committed, when it—and correctly—recognized human development as a product of adaptability, but cut off this adaptability by death, and yet could believe that the product of adaptability can be deposited in Zoosperms and be inherited above the physiological material value."

In January, 1904, I lived a short time in the Hotel La Pintoresca at Pasadena,* which can be reached in three-quarters of an hour from Los Angeles by the electric car. It is situated directly among the mountains; but even during this month I suffered from the terrible heat; yet the thermometer usually showed from 86 to 90

---

*On the occasion of visiting a school, the teacher, when I introduced myself as a "German," had the *Lorelei* sung for me by children seven or eight years old, among them several negroes, in faultless German, with no American accent.

degrees till three in the afternoon, and there was no rain. I had hoped gradually to acclimatize myself to Southern California, but I had now been a year and a half in this climate and suffered no less than at first in this half-tropical region. It is true, as acquaintances consoled me by saying, that one can make snow-balls, gather roses, and take a sea-bath on the same day; but one cannot be always "in the car." Mount Lowe, the refuge of the residents of Los Angeles, is reached in about two hours, in connection with which I will remark that the car system in California is much better developed than, for instance, in Berlin, especially as concerns comfort and speed. Snow can be found on the slopes of the Sierra Nevada, whose summit is reached by a cog-wheel road. Returning from there, one reaches in about an hour Pasadena, which in January displays magnificent roses and where, as in Los Angeles, the orange and lemon orchards ripen their fruit in January. From Pasadena one can go by way of Los Angeles in about two hours to Santa Monica or Redondo or Long Beach (all three on the Pacific Ocean), where one can bathe in the open sea in January or take a little voyage to Santa Catalina Island, a romantic isle in the sea, like Heligoland or Capri.* Rowboats, with a glass bottom, permit a view of the floor of the sea, which displays a fairy-like splendour in its plant formations, amid which swim throngs of gold fish and other species. Only on the Lake of Garda in 1896, and later on the road along the Mediterranean, between Nice and Villa Franca, have I seen anything like it. I brought cones seventeen inches long from the pine trees on the snow-clad mountains and adorned my room with them. As California borders upon Mexico, I did not wish to miss seeing this country, especially as the feeling was maturing in my mind that I must soon turn northward on account of the climate; so, on the 25th of January, 1904, I set out on the journey.

I left Los Angeles on Monday, and did not arrive in the city of Mexico until Friday. The long ride across Arizona and New Mexico to the frontier station of El Paso in Texas, led

---

*I remember with great pleasure Capri, where I lived at Pagano in 1886. At that time life had not yet made me the phenomenal pessimist—in contrast to the transcendental optimist. My experiences and conflicts with the mire of the world did not begin until 1888.

everywhere through prairies. At El Paso there is a change of road, and then the journey continues two more days and nights over similar prairies, though in the distance the mountains of the Sierra Madre and the Cordilleras of the coast are constantly in view. In the city of Mexico, however, I stayed at the Hotel Iturbide—one feels richly rewarded for these fatiguing experiences. A really charming city, thoroughly clean, and built with much architectural magnificence in the new portion. Everything there is nearly one-half cheaper than in the United States; the climate, too, is much more agreeable than in Southern California; yet it lies at a height of nearly 7500 feet, so that it is never too hot and never too cool. Before the "Presidium," now occupied by the President, which for nearly three years served as the residence of poor Archduke Maximilian of Austria, who was shot on the 19th of June, 1867, I remembered the castle of Miramar at Trieste, with its marvellously beautiful situation, which I visited in 1902, on my way to Egypt. In this castle, a Mexican deputation offered the tempting imperial crown to the unfortunate Habsburg, which solemn event is commemorated in a large oil painting hanging in Miramar.

From Central Mexico one travels probably hundreds of miles through plantations of agaves, from whose leaves, nearly as thick as one's fist, the Mexicans prepare their national drink "pulque," a syrup-like white mass whose taste was not agreeable to me. In order to see a genuine tropical landscape, I resolved to go to Vera Cruz, on the Gulf of Mexico, along which road one can most readily become acquainted with the tropics. I did not regret it. Orizaba, Jalapa, and Puebla were recommended to me. I had already seen the beauties of the tropics in Southern Egypt and Nubia, and shall never forget the brilliant starry sky arching above the ruins of the Temple of Ammon of the Pharaohs in Karnak, opposite ancient Thebes, or a wonderful tropical night in Assouan in the Libyan desert, but there one finds no vegetation except palms and cacti. On this route, however, I was to see tropical forests in their full indescribable majesty. In Orizaba I stood marvelling in the midst of the sugarcane, coffee, tobacco, and banana plantations. It was the first of February, 1904; the sugarcane had just been cut, and the coffee trees were full of beans. I am not botanist enough to give the names of all the plants and trees which this tropical climate produces: Mimosas, the logwood tree, figs, bamboos, palms, bignonias, mahogany,* and hundreds of other species, all growing wild together, with a magnificence of blossom that mocks description! Dozens of vultures attend to the cleanliness by devouring every animal that dies there; I have seen them myself eagerly sucking up the warm blood of a slaughtered steer.

In Jalapa, Vera Cruz, on the Gulf of Mexico, the same picture. The common people in Mexico, it is true, are backward in civilization; in the flat country one usually sees nothing but clay huts, similar to the dirty clay dwellings of the fellaheen on the Nile.

As my time was limited, I could not look into occultism in Mexico, though Max Rahn, editor of *"Die Uebersinnliche Welt,"* Berlin, by his valuable compilation of nearly all of the occult societies and publications in the whole

---

*The fruits of the pomegranate and cherimoya have a wonderfully delicious flavour. The bananas here are red, while the Jamaica banana, which is most eaten in America, is yellow.

world, has materially lightened the traveller's task in quickly finding the persons connected with such matters, even though many addresses, principally in the English and Spanish speaking countries through which I have travelled, were no longer to be found.

It is interesting that, in America, I met a number of trance mediums, who instantly told me—and correctly—from what little physical illness I was suffering. When I think of the year 1898, when a Jewish physician denounced me in Berlin because I was said to have made somnambulistic diagnoses, which, in the case alleged by him, was not true, a feeling of regret comes over me at the knowledge of how far behind other countries, including my native German land, still remain in the so-called province of the occult science, or if one will have it so, in the perception of *odic intermingling and sensitiveness of feeling.*

Mme. de Thèbes in Paris, whom I visited for the first time in 1900, told me at once, after she had examined the lines of my hand, that I suffered from rheumatism, which was true. This was a brilliant demonstration, for the science of chiromancy or palmistry is unknown in Germany, at least in the so-called exact scientific circles.

As early as 1839, Dr. Frappart proposed to utilize the medicinal powers of somnambulists, in order to test the infinitely small doses of medicaments, with the remark that this "intuitive medicine" would overthrow all the systems of physicians.* When will the time at last come when the "men of science" will study the works of du Prel? One of his latest books† presents a compilation in regard to this, which will make his name forever remembered.

I know a Chinese physician in Los Angeles —there is a Chinese and a Mexican quarter, where only Chinese and Mexicans live—who makes diagnoses solely by the pulse, and accurately. He lays two fingers on the patient's pulse, and instantly names the disease without going into a trance.

---

*Frappart: *Lettres sur le magnétisme et le somnambulisme* (Letters on Magnetism and Somnambulism), p. 152. See Willy Reichel in *Brockhaus Konversations-Lexikon* (Brockhaus' Encyclopedia), *Psychical Studies*, 1901, p. 213, and Baron von Reichenbach: *Der sensitive Mensch* (The sensitive human being), Stuttgart, 1854, I, p. 428.

†Dr. Carl du Prel: *Die Magie als Naturwissenschaft* (Magic as a Natural Science), Jena, 1899, and *Die Entdeckung der Seele* (The Discovery of the Soul), Leipzig, 1894-95.

Of course there is also plenty of swindling in America. But Passavant* is right in saying: "These powers would be abused, like all powers in the world, the highest, the most horrible. But call all history to witness, ask all the generations of the earth, whose skeletons are in the soil on which we walk: Has ever any great and glorious apparition manifested itself to the world, even where the hand of the Eternal visibly touched the earth, which was not laughed at by shallowness, deformed by superstition, gnawed like a worm by mockery, and darkened, abused, poisoned by the gloomy spirit of falsehood? But is it due to the water, that the lily draws from its fragrance, and the hemlock poison?"

At the end of February, 1904, I had occasion to visit San Francisco again. A friend, an American colonel, obtained passage for me on the government boat, which goes around San Francisco Bay several times daily to carry provisions and convey the mail to the different fortifications. This bay makes a far more romantic impression than New York harbour; it

---

*Dr. J. C. Passavant: *Investigations of Magnetism and Clairvoyance*, Frankfort, 1821, p. 20.

is encircled by mountains and peopled by countless sea-lions, which can be seen best from Cliff House.

I then again visited Mr. Miller, to have new experiences, which made me earnestly wish that Colonel de Rochas, or Professor Charles Richet, or Camille Flammarion in Paris, or the Society for Psychical Research in London could scientifically test this medium. Miller was born in Nancy (France) on the 8th of September, 1870, and has been for fourteen years in America; I regret extremely that Professor Zöllner, du Prel, and Baron Hellenbach are already snatched from this earthly sphere, for in Miller these leaders in the occult domain in Germany would have found great delight. Miller will visit France again in 1906, and I heard from Professor van der Naillen, the President of the School of Engineering in San Francisco, who is a friend of de Rochas, that he would call the attention of the latter tried investigator to Miller. Any one who is an expert in occultism knows that, if one has several seances with the same medium, they always improve, if sympathy and harmony have existed.

I will now—except in one case, which I must

treat more in detail—briefly state what I experienced with Miller. I saw, by an amply sufficient light, while Miller was standing before the curtain, a fully developed spirit come out from behind it, go about nine feet, to a lady sitting beside me, embrace and kiss her—it was his mother—and then watched Mr. Miller who —not in a trance—slowly followed him, as he took him by the hand and led him back to the curtain, where he dematerialized before it. I also saw eight times a gentleman well known to me in life, ten feet away from the medium, first approaching and sinking in front of me as a little floating flame, develop in perhaps a minute and a half, till he stood in his full figure directly before my eyes. He then held long conversations with me, drew back himself to the curtain, where I followed, and dematerialized himself before my eyes, still talking until his head at last vanished.

This spirit, in his voice and his whole manner of speech, was absolutely unmistakable; but as he developed himself in white robes, I asked him if he would be able, that is, if he could remember in what dress he was laid in the coffin, and to materialize in this for a still more positive proof of identity. He promised to do so, and came the next day to a seance in a dress-coat, exactly as I had seen him in the coffin, his face without any covering. I saw with my own eyes little revolving flames, white, blue, and a wonderful light-blue, from which voices spoke to me, giving their full names, and those of friends and relatives; some sank and quickly developed, but others had not yet attained this ability. I saw my nephew Helmuth, who died in Berlin, August 31st, 1898, as a child four years old, float with his fair hair out of the cabinet, calling constantly: "Uncle, do you see me?" I saw him hovering about in the room a long time and then disappearing through the ceiling.* Who, having had such an experience fall to his lot even once, which makes all farther proofs superfluous, could still doubt the truth of Spiritualism? I saw and heard these things several times.

On another occasion, at a private seance,

---

*Concerning a disappearance through the ceiling of a room Professor Perty reports with the medium Williams in London in his book, *Der jetzige Spiritualismus und verwandte Erfahrungen* (Modern Spiritualism and Kindred Experiences), Leipzig, 1877, p. 164, as well as Florence Marryat in *There is no Death*, p. 342, with the medium Virginia Roberts.

standing directly behind Miller, who was not in a trance, I saw bright flames floating from every direction from which voices addressed me in the most touching manner. I saw at a public seance, for at least twelve minutes, a spirit, fully materialized, sit among us and talk with us. I saw at least a dozen spirits develop before those attending the seance, usually two or three yards from the medium who, meanwhile, was talking unconcernedly several times; and heard rappings, which sometimes echoed like cannonading; also other tests, for instance: bringing back a watch that had been lost six years, I will mention only incidentally, as the materialization was so amazing, that all the rest recedes into the background by comparison.

Miller possesses no less than eight "Controls." "Betsy" is the principal one. She has hard work, but she is tireless and a dear, kind spirit. This spirit was a servant of the medium's grandparents; she was a negress, and, as she says, has undertaken this hard mission out of gratitude for the good treatment which she received from them. Another is an Indian Star Eagle—who possesses medical knowledge, and who explained to me in detail my illness, whose

An Occultist's Travels. 45

original cause no physician had yet found, while, fully materialized, he himself placed the remedy for it in my hand.

I will not enter farther into the conversations with these spirits, as they principally concerned private affairs, and I do not occupy myself with spiritualistic revelations. I am in general of the same opinion as du Prel: "There is as yet no spiritualism which opens up to us the real world beyond the grave, but only one which teaches us to know the phenomena occurring between the two worlds."*

If any one has an interest in the revelations of the world beyond the grave, the works of Swedenborg, Cahagnet, Dr. Friese, A. J. Davis, Hudson Tuttle, Allan Kardec, Annie Besant, Mme. d'Espérance, and others are at his disposal.†

I must describe more fully one incident at Miller's—I have already alluded to it—because

---

*Du Prel: *Der Tod, das Jenseits, das Leben im Jenseits* (Death, the World Beyond, the Life in the World Beyond), Munich, 1899, p. 301.

† The *Kundgebungen des Geistes Emanuel* (Demonstrations of the Spirit Emanuel), 1890-1897, collected by B. Forsboom, a friend of du Prel (published by Karl Siegismund in Berlin) are the most sympathetic to me of "spiritualist revelations."

I cannot recollect having read anything similar in the more recent spiritualist literature; and this is a dematerialization of a living human being and the finding him again in another story. The magnificent pamphlet by Dr. Walter Bormann, *"The Scotchman Home"* (Leipzig, O. Mutze, 1899), describes the levitations of Home, but not the dissolving of his whole body. Du Prel,* too, has compiled a large number of levitations of all periods, but I cannot recall having read there of the disappearance of a living person, as took place in Miller's case.†

The incident occurred in the following manner: Mr. Miller was sitting in the cabinet, in a trance, and Betsy summoned me into the cabinet in order to convince myself that Miller was sleeping in it. She called me the "German gentleman." The seance this time consisted of twenty-seven persons. She said to me: "We will now dematerialize our medium and remove

---

*Du Prel: *Die Magic als Naturwissenschaft* (Magic as a Natural Science), Jena, 1899, p. 147.

†Subsequently I found a report of a disappearance of a medium by William Eglinton, so the "Miller" case does not stand alone. See *Animismus und Spiritismus* (Animism and Spiritualism), by A. Aksakow, 2d edition, II, p. 288, and Vesme, *Geschichte des Spiritismus* (History of Spiritualism), Leipsic, O, Mutze, 1898, II, p. 127.

him to the second story, and you and another gentleman and two ladies must get the key to the second story and bring the medium down again."

I will mention that the whole house belongs to Mr. Miller, and the seances were held on the ground floor, while the second story, as Miller is not married, is kept securely locked, since thieving is not rare in California. Betsy also requested us to join hands and sing, in order to obtain perfect calmness of soul, and the greatest harmony, because her purpose was extremely difficult. I again carefully examined everything, convinced myself that it would have been utterly impossible for Miller to get out of the cabinet, since twenty-seven persons were sitting directly in front of it and there was abundant light, while the back of the cabinet faced directly upon the street. Even if a window should be opened—there was no door—any draught of air, and besides, it was stormy, rainy weather, would have been instantly noticed by us. After about four minutes, Betsy's voice was heard, asking that we four persons should now go. I had the housekeeper, who was sitting in the circle, give me the key, and we went to the second story, where I unlocked the door, and really found Mr. Miller, breathing heavily, sitting in a chair. I took the medium, who was still in a trance, by the hand and led him back into our circle, where he awoke without any recollection of what had happened; only his heart gave him pain.

When the question of the fourth dimension of space was brought up by Professor Zöllner of Leipzig, Lazar von Hellenbach asked his medium the question whether a human being could disappear by the way of the fourth dimension. The answer was: "A human being could under certain circumstances. There is too much respect for it, to do it often, but there are cases where human beings disappeared and became invisible to their persecutors, as Christ in the Temple." Thanks to the philosophical works of Hellenbach* and du Prel, the idea of personality has obtained an entirely new development, so that the difficulties which the spiritualistic problem presents to us, are now, to a large extent, removed.

We now know that our inner (individual)

---

*Hellenbach: *Vorurtheile der Menschheit* (Prejudices of Mankind), Leipzig, 1884, II, p. 273.

consciousness and our outer (sense) consciousness are not one and the same thing—experiments in the provinces of somnambulism and hypnotism prove this truth—that our personality, which is the result of our outer consciousness, cannot be identified with the Ego which belongs to our inner consciousness, or, to put it briefly, that what we call our self-consciousness is not the equivalent of our inner consciousness. So we must distinguish between the personality and the individuality. The individuality endures, the personality vanishes. That is why the question of the identity of the spirits is the stumbling block of spiritualism, and for that very reason cases of this kind, which stand the test, are so extremely rare. That is also the reason that the communications through mediums can give us no definite disclosures concerning the Spirit World and its inhabitants; the transcendental world is just as immeasurable an idea to the phenomenal world as the conception of the fourth dimension; we can have no idea of it.

But I can now assert, with all positiveness, that at Mr. Miller's I saw three spirits undoubtedly in their outer form, without any muffling, and recognized them by their speech to be the departed persons whose names they gave. Of course, Miller has had a great deal written about him in the American professional press, as well as in the daily papers. I have read more or less detailed descriptions of him in *The Better Way, The Searchlight, Light of Truth, Philosophical Journal, Rays of Truth, Examiner* (a daily paper appearing in San Francisco, which gave full description of a seance of the Russian Grand Duke Boris with Miller), etc.; but I wish, as I have already remarked, that this medium might become known in scientific circles in Europe, in order surely to be one of the best corner-stones for the erection of the doctrine of the truth of transcendental intercourse with our departed friends.

I have experienced many other things with Miller; for instance, once two spirits materialized who said that they had been Egyptian dancing-girls; they wound up themselves a musical clock standing beside me, and danced, that is, made the dancing movements, similar to those I had seen the dancing dervishes perform in Cairo in January, 1902, after which they dematerialized before my eyes.

An Occultist's Travels.

Another time beings appeared, shining radiantly from within outward—words of description fail me—they said that they had never lived upon this earth, but were "Spirits of the Sun," and allowed me to touch them, in order to convince me that, out of love for mankind, they had adapted themselves for this moment to the earthly sphere.

Women spirits appeared, with children in their arms, such as Professor Perty describes in his account of experiences with the Eddy medium in Chittenden (Vermont, America). Professor Perty has collected a great number of similar experiences in this interesting province.*

---

*Professor Dr. Perty: *Der jetzige Spiritualismus und verwandte Erscheinungen* (Modern Spiritualism and Kindred Experiences), Leipzig and Heidelberg, 1877; *Die sichtbare und die unsichtbare Welt* (The Visible and the Invisible World), 1881; *Blicke in das verborgene Gebiet des Menschengeistes* (Glimpses of the Hidden Domain of the Human Spirit), 1869; Vesme, *Geschichte des Spiritismus* (History of Spiritualism), Leipsic, O. Mutze, 1898, and Carl Kiesewetter: *Geschichte des neueren Okkultismus* (History of Modern Occultism), Leipsic, Wilhelm Friedrich, 1891.

III.

Mr. Miller visited me in April, 1904, in Los Angeles, where I was then residing, about five hundred miles from San Francisco. On his arrival I examined him, as well as his two pieces of hand-luggage, and built a cabinet myself in my own private dwelling; but again, as at the first seance, behind my chair five feet away from the medium—the same spirit that I have previously fully described, developed himself in shining robes. Then a female spirit came out of the cabinet, went through the door into the entry, about thirty feet away, and blessed the house. Other spirits, with whose works I had occupied myself years ago, appeared and greeted me in the most cordial manner. The most striking thing with Miller is that all these spirits instantly mentioned their names—Christian and surnames—and with an accuracy which I never before experienced.

In a word, these seances in my own residence

An Occultist's Travels. 53

presented the same phenomena as those in San Francisco. In everything I am writing down here I am perfectly aware of the full significance of my words.

It is very probable that many readers would like to learn what interesting things the spirits momentarily materialized through the intervention of so unusually highly-endowed a medium have communicated to me concerning the life after death. I have heard much, for spirits reported themselves by their full names, who had formerly represented the most diverse ideas in their works; but the relative value of these statements, in my opinion, is to be accepted very critically, since, according to experience, they contradict themselves with different mediums. Professor Zöllner has given this warning in vigorous language.*

In the seances with Miller I heard the spirits speak only English, French, and German, but I was several times assured that, in a seance of seventy-five persons, which was held shortly before, twenty-seven languages and dialects

---

*Professor Zöllner: *Die transzendentale Physik* (Transcendental Physics), III, Leipzig, 1879, Preface, p. 36.

were spoken by the spirits, corresponding with the number of the various nationalities that, no rarity in San Francisco, were present. Professor Zöllner, on April 28th, 1879, wrote the following warning to his friend, Dr. Friese, in Breslau:

"Science can do nothing with the purport of intellectual revelations, but must continue its structure by the guidance of observed facts and the conclusions logically and mathematically uniting them. If we forsake this path, we shall inevitably fall into the theological and philosophical wrangling of scholars about the substance and origin of historically transmitted assertions. We should once more experience the same dissension between the various adherents of individual revelations that history has handed down to us in blood-stained characters in the religious battles of former times." The power of suggestion of these mediums is immensely great!

I myself have noticed a case with Miller, which, without doubt, rested solely upon telepathy. Thomson Jay Hudson has written a book,*

---

*Thomson Jay Hudson: *The Law of Psychical Phenomena.*

An Occultist's Travels. 55

which was translated into German by Eduard Herman.

In many things I do not agree with him, but I advise every one who desires to avoid the cliffs and the undeniable perils of Spiritualism, to study industriously this work of a connoisseur in the doubtful province.

Meanwhile, the United States had opened the World's Fair in St. Louis, which, on the 1st of June, 1904, I set out to visit. St. Louis is reached from Los Angeles in four days by the Santa Fé railroad, through Arizona, New Mexico, Colorado, Kansas, and Missouri, as far as Kansas almost everywhere through prairies! I have now gradually passed through the endless plains of grass, whose view, according to Schopenhauer (The Platonic Idea: "The Object of Art") is famed for its impression of sublimity, from the Atlantic to the Pacific, and from the Mexican frontier to Canada; yet upon me they have always made a melancholy impression.

I can omit describing the Exposition; all the newspapers in the world were full of it; personally, I was most pleased with the Japanese, and then with the German, exhibit. On the way through Arizona, I branched off to the Grand Cañon. The accessible part of this immense gorge has a length of two hundred and seventeen miles, and a vertical depth of about 6000 feet, and is thirteen miles wide at the point from which visitors generally view it. The author of "Etidorpha"* ought to have had his journey to the Under World commence here.

I remained at the World's Fair, from the 5th to the 12th of June, at the Inside Inn Hotel, which was in the exhibition grounds, and then took the Burlington route through Nebraska and Montana to reach, in two days and a half, the Yellowstone Park in Wyoming. This tract was made a national park in 1872; it is about sixty-two miles long, fifty-four miles wide, and has an area of thirty-three thousand and twelve square miles. The trip through this vast "Paradise"—in the Greek sense of the word—is made by stage in five and a half days. I saw there the buffalo, the elk, the bear, etc., in full liberty; but as these animals are not hunted here, even the bear approaches within about two hundred yards of human beings; at the "Fountain

---

Etidorpha or The End of the World, by John Uri Lloyd.

Hotel," I saw three bears that had come down from the mountains trot along and, after finding the food which the hotel daily throws out for them, quickly disappear in the forests. But the principal objects of interest in Yellowstone Park are the geysers, periodical hot springs, of which the Giant rises two hundred and fifty feet. There are about thirty-three of the most noteworthy, which spout at intervals of from five minutes to twelve days, lasting from one to ninety minutes. In a large portion of this park one walks upon cold sulphur; there is a boiling and a bubbling everywhere, like a pool in Hades, and I could not help being vividly reminded of Dante and his "Divine Comedy." On a very small scale I had witnessed something similar in 1886 in the Solfatarra at Pozzuoli, near Naples, and on the Lake of Garda at Sermione, where the villa of the Roman poet Catullus once stood. (In July, 1896, I lived at Maderno on the Lake of Garda, in which month the Italian portion of this lake displays its full magnificence. I most admired the caper tree and the passion flowers.) The wood near the Norris Hotel, where the sulphur has turned the trees perfectly white, so that it seems as though one were in a petrified forest, is also very interesting.

To return from Yellowstone Park I took the Northern Pacific road by way of Idaho, Washington, and Oregon, to California. This journey reconciled me again to many things in America. The days of travel through those endless prairies of Central America were always depressing to my mind, but the trip from Livingston to Portland, Ore., and then southward to San Francisco, is thoroughly charming. The Rocky Mountains and the Cascade Mountains, the spurs of the Sierra Nevada, which one crosses, are incomparably more beautiful than the mountains through which the Union Pacific passes farther south. Everywhere there are lakes and rivers and snow-clad peaks—so for nearly four days one travels through perfectly magnificent scenery.

On arriving again in San Francisco, it was naturally a matter of course that I sought Mr. Miller and had about twelve seances with him. The phenomena were almost the same, with the exception of one case, which aroused my eager interest. I might mention in advance, that the spirits which, in his circle, are distinguished as high," represent the theory of palingenesis, or reincarnation, not in the sense of the esoteric doctrine of Buddhism, but in the sense of Allan Kardec. I will not touch here upon the much-disputed question of reincarnation from the standpoint of its spiritual value—it certainly sounds plausible—but it must not be overlooked that Miller is a Frenchman, and that, according to experience, mediums are very easily accessible to the psychologization of preconceived ideas and that occult France probably contains the largest number of believers in Kardec's reincarnation theory.

Privy-Councillor Aksakov, as is well known, has stated the following scheme for materialization: "Visible and complete materialization of a whole human form corresponds with a complete and maximal dematerialization of the medium to the point where he may become invisible," which phenomenon he describes in detail in his "Psychical Studies,"* Leipzig, Germany.

I have witnessed with Miller a similar, very

---

*A phenomenon making an epoch in the province of materialization, *Psychical Studies,* 1894, p. 284, etc.; see *Animismus und Spiritismus* (Animism and Spiritualism), 2d edition, p. 264-266.

remarkable phenomenon. I asked a spirit, whom I have already mentioned, and who repeatedly embraced and kissed me, to try whether I could see him at the same time with the medium. In a seance of twenty-two persons he appeared fully materialized and beside him the medium bare from the head to the waist. In less than three minutes, however, the medium's head became like a child's, then diminished still more, and finally became invisible. If Mr. Miller should visit France and England, I hope that he will find conditions there which will enable theoretically and practically trained investigators, like de Rochas, Richet, and others, to see similar things under strict test conditions.

On the 3d of July I reached Los Angeles again, but I did not feel happy there. Without refined society, without intellectual pleasures, I often fell into dull indifference or a morbid state of excitement. I remember once having read "Chips of Thought" by Maxim Gorki, which apply to me exactly; they run approximately as follows: "The more sensitive a man is, the less energy there is in him, the more he suffers and the harder his life is. Solitude and longing are the destiny of such human beings!"

An Occultist's Travels.

As the heat in Southern California this year was unusually great, on the 26th of July I again took refuge in the mountains with my friend Ralph Follows in the San Gabriel cañon, this time with my Winchester rifle and Nietzsches' "Zarathustra." I admire this artist in style, though his view of life, from the ethical standpoint, is diametrically opposed to mine.

Kardec, too, I read here again after an interval of years, Dr. du Prel is also a representative of the reincarnation theory, and Baron Hellenbach at least does not reject it. True, it cannot be absolutely proved; but, as already remarked, to every consistent logician it sounds very acceptable. In reply to a question in regard to this asked at Miller's, as to how I myself stood in this respect, I received the answer that I was already reincarnated for the fourth time. The last time—about three hundred years ago—I had been a Bohemian king, who desired as such to give his people laws which would lead to progress, but he could not accomplish it, and therefore died discontented and weary of life; I had now reincarnated myself again to serve mankind by the dissemination of magnetism and occultism. It is true that I was born of a family which, on both the paternal and maternal side, possessed magnetic and mediumistic powers. My grandfather* was, as previously mentioned, a highly esteemed physician and strong magnetizer in his time, and my father's sister was a psychographic medium, so that I seem to have inherited my gift of sensitiveness.

It all sounds thoroughly possible, and whoever is familiar with the intellectual essays on this subject by Dr. Hübbe-Schleiden in the "Sphinx," Brunswick, Germany, would perhaps reject the opinion of A. J. Davis,† who uncere-

---

*Dr. Julius Neuberth became in 1847 a member of the Kaiser Leopold-Carol Academy of Naturalists in Halle, and his *Original Beiträge zur Geschichte des Somnambulismus* (Original Contributions to the History of Somnambulism), Leipzig, Otto Wigand, 1841, was quoted by Du Prel in *Die Magie als Naturwissenschaft,* Jena, Costenoble, 1899, p. 148. He also wrote *Die Heilkraft der menschlichen Hand* (The Healing Power of the Human Hand), Grimma, 1843, and numerous essays in the *Dresdner Wochenblatt* (Dresden Weekly). At that time he had a difficult position, for Magnetism was still very little known. Count Szapary was almost the only person who supported him.

†See A. J. Davis, *Spiritual Journeys* and *Principles of Nature.* I am thoroughly acquainted with *The Esoteric Doctrine,* by Sinnett; *The Sea of Theosophy,* by W. Q. Judge; *Buddistischer Katechismus* (Buddhist Catechism), by Subhadra Bickshu, Brunswick, 1888; *Light on the Path,* by Mabel Collins, and *Bhagavad Gita,* Brunswick, 1892, in the edition of Dr. Franz Hartmann.

moniously declared the reincarnation to be a jest of the "Diakka." But, on the other hand, what Aksakov has written concerning the genesis of Kardec's works, gives food for thought.*

---

*Investigations of the Historical Origin of the Reincarnation Dogmas in French Spiritualism, by A. Aksakov; Psychical Studies, 1898, p. 258. See also: The Origin of Life and Spirit, by A. Voss; Uebersinnliche Welt (Transcendental World), p. 343. For the rest, the controlling spirits of the Banner of Light (Boston, Mass.), have always represented the theory of reincarnation, that is also in America. See Ludwig Deinhard, Amerikanischer Spiritualismus (American Spiritualism), Sphinx (Gera, Reuss), 1890, p. 75, in his criticism of Henry Lacroix, the Paris correspondent of the Banner of Light.

IV.

In Europe, as well as in America, I have known men of high culture and noble character and noticed that they often obtained nothing at seances, while I supposed that high-mindedness and magnanimity ought to induce good sittings. It was positively painful to me to see such persons, after I had made every effort to convince them of the transcendental life, leave seances with mediums who were usually excellent, unsatisfied. Hellenbach gives a very acceptable explanation: "The fixed destiny of a human being may also be an obstacle. Man comes into the world for some purpose of development; if this goal is inconsistent with his taking up this branch of knowledge, there will be mutual repugnance between him and it. As instinct guides animals in the interest of food, so an inward impulse guides man to the search for the necessary factors in his ethical development. It is perfectly conceivable that the unseen intelligences feel a certain aversion to interfering with certain personalities."*

I hope later to be able to put in book form my experiences in the transcendental domain with many mediums. I have so many to note which utterly preclude the idea of a masked telepathy (and therein lies the "Punctum saliens").

True, the Berlin "Philosopher of the Unknown," Eduard von Hartmann, once said to my brother that nothing in the world would be more horrible to him than the thought of a continued life, and the Jena zoologist, Professor Dr. Ernst Haeckel, calls the common conception of eternal life no glorious consolation, but a terrible menacing outlook. (*Die Weltratsel*, Bonn, 1899, p. 240.)

But if there is a personally conscious continued life and for my own part I cannot doubt it, death will lose its terrors, since it will then be only a relative birth, just as the earthly birth is a relative death; for while in the latter the transcendental subject recedes into obscurity to

---

*Hellenbach: *Geburt und Tod* (Birth and Death), Vienna, 1885, p. 237, 2d edition, Leipzig, O. Mutze, 1907.

our cerebral consciousness, in death it will again become free.

In a precisely similar sense, Kant has already said in his *Lecture on Metaphysics:* "Death is not the absolute ending of life, but a liberation from the obstacles to a complete life."

Wonderfully beautiful, therefore, are the words of the motto which I found in Professor Zöllner's works:

"The highest thing which thy spirit seeks to draw from the eternal source of all existence is but an image."*

It has often happened to me, as it probably has to every trained experimenter in this province, with mediums through whom I spoke to spiritual beings and also saw them fully materialized and believed I recognized them as the persons they announced themselves to be, that afterwards they said something which again awakened doubts of their identity in my mind.

Hermann Handrich in Brooklyn, who has had especially numerous experiences in this

---

*Professor Zöllner: *Wissenschaftliche Abhandlungen* (Scientific Essays), II, Part I, p. 435; *Kepler und die unsichtbare Welt* (Kepler and the Invisible World), Leipzig, 1878.

province, describes similar things.* An American physician, an Agnostic, who, as I believed, had seen in my house unobjectionable materializations, told me that these phenomena were contradictory to the known laws of Nature, and did not even interest him! Yet, as the discoverer of thallium, Professor Sir W. Crookes, Fellow of the Royal Society in London, † says: "It is evident that the facts are of the most amazing character and seem wholly irreconcilable with all the theories of modern science. After I have convinced myself of the truth, it would be a moral cowardice to withhold my testimony." I do not understand how a man can be so presumptuous as to believe that he knows all the laws of Nature.

It is certainly easy to understand that a scientist, who has created a solid base for himself, on which he has erected his knowledge, and who then suddenly sees that a new discovery is threatening to undermine that foundation, does not find this exactly agreeable, for

---

*Hermann Handrich: *Erfahrungs-Reflexionem* (Reflections on Experiences), *Psychical Studies*, 1901, p. 713.
†W. Crookes: *Notes of an Investigation into Spiritual Phenomena, Psychical Studies.*

which reason so many representatives of the science of the schools play an ostrich policy; even Professor Virchow, *Ueber Wunder* ("About Miracles"), p. 23, says: "We do not rejoice to see a new phenomenon; on the contrary, it is often painful." Cremonini da Cento, Libri, Clavius, Magini, Horky, genuine "men of science," refused to look through the telescope, because they thought they must, on theoretical grounds, deny the existence of Jupiter's four moons.

As has been previously mentioned, I had published in the number of the *"Revue Spirite"* (Paris), appearing August, 1904, certain things about the medium Miller. In January, 1905, I heard from San Francisco that a letter had come from Valence-sur-Rhône to Mr. Miller, from a gentleman, J. Debrus, requesting him to give twelve seances for de Rochas, himself, and several friends, because I had remarked that Miller would visit France again in 1905. My wish was fulfilled in so far as Colonel Count de Rochas desired to see Mr. Miller. So, full of good cheer, I went to San Francisco to try what was to be done, and with the intention of eventually accompanying Mr. Miller to Paris. But I

An Occultist's Travels. 69

did not find Mr. Miller in the best state of mind, as certain recent psychical excitements had made him somewhat nervous. His controls told me that he could not go to Paris under four or five months, and on account of the sudden change of atmosphere, and other conditions in France, I must not expect such wonderful seances as in California; but perhaps M. de Rochas might be persuaded to come here.

To accomplish this, I was obliged to make other arrangements. I put myself into communication with Professor van der Naillen, a friend of de Rochas, who met me in the most cordial manner. A seance arranged on the same evening, where van der Naillen saw the medium Miller at the same time with two fully materialized phantoms, was permitted to touch them, and other things induced him to give me his support in every way, in order to persuade de Rochas, in the interest of occultism and humanity, to accept my invitation. In order to lead the latter investigator to do this, that is, to be able to send him a report which might induce him to undertake this long journey, we were obliged to forward to him a report of a test seance under absolutely conclusive and unobjectionable conditions, with signatures from persons of scientific reputation.

After Mr. Miller had given his consent with the words: "Do with me as you please," Professor van der Naillen called in as a third, Dr. Renz, a universally esteemed German physician, and we agreed what tests we must require. I first bought a new black shirt, black under vest and trousers, then ordered a new suit for Miller, and had these articles sent directly to the Palace Hotel, where I was living, so that Miller did not see them before the seance. I then hired at the Palace Hotel—it is the most aristocratic one in San Francisco—a second room, whose selection I left to Professor van der Naillen, and had the cabinet constructed of black material by an upholsterer. On the 2nd of February this test seance took place. Besides Dr. Renz and his wife, Dr. Burgess, Professor Braunwalder, Professor of Electricity at the School of Engineering in San Francisco, Mr. Charles Dawbarn, the Californian philosopher, the Turkish consul, and other prominent persons who had accepted our invitation were present.

Mr. Miller appeared in the hotel at half past eight o'clock, received by van der Naillen, Dr.

Renz, and myself. We took him to my room, where before our eyes, he undressed entirely and put on the articles of clothing already mentioned. Then we went into the seance room, where Professor van der Naillen and Dr. Renz bound the medium with strong ropes, previously purchased, by his arms, hands, chest, neck, and feet, three or four times to a chair, and sewed the ends fast to the carpeted floor. The room was about forty feet above the street. During the whole seance Miller was not in a trance and the cabinet was almost always open. In spite of these difficult conditions, nine phantoms gradually materialized sometimes ten or twelve feet from the medium. Betsy, the principal control spirit, went away so far that Mr. Miller called: "Betsy, come back, I am suffering terribly."

I received later from Professor van der Naillen a very long and full report in the French language, which, with a letter of introduction from myself to de Rochas, I sent to Paris to be forwarded. There was not one in this seance of sixteen persons, among whom were several avowed skeptics, who did not become convinced of the genuineness of the phenomena by this sitting under such conditions.

At a seance, held three days later, at Mr. Miller's house, something occurred so interesting that I would not like to pass it over. The sitting took place at noon. Before it began, and while Mr. Miller was standing in front of the cabinet, I heard Betsy's voice whisper: "Go out into the sun with the professor a moment." I took Mr. Miller by the arm and went with him into the street, which was reached directly from the room by merely opening a door, after which we immediately returned. At the moment we entered the dark room, I and all present saw Mr. Miller completely strewn with a shining, white, glittering mass like snow, that entirely covered his dark cheviot suit. I have witnessed this singular occurrence several times; even when he had not previously been in the sun, even for a moment, his clothing, as soon as the room was darkened, gradually appeared covered with snow. This is evidently the white element of magnetism which the phantoms use in their development, as distinguished from the blue, which is effective in healing operations.

It is more difficult for phantoms to appear in the garments which they wore in life, because they must take these materials from those present, while—so they told me—they could find the "white magnetism" in the atmosphere. In the seances at Miller's I almost always felt, just before the appearance of the phantoms, the well known almost icy breath of air, which has been so often described in test sittings.

On April 12th, 1905, I received Colonel de Rochas' answer. Since it might be of considerable interest, I will give it in his wording:

GRENOBLE, March 27th, 1905.
MONSIEUR LE PROFESSEUR:

Please pardon my long delay in answering your letter of February 11th, 1905; but it did not reach me until the 6th of March, and I was then in my bed from the effects of a violent attack of grippe, from which I am only gradually beginning to recover.

In the present condition of my health, it is impossible for me to foresee when I shall be able to expose myself to the fatigue of so long a journey, even made under the arrangements you so kindly offer me.

I am, however, strongly tempted; for, like you, I am devoting all the energy I possess in trying to raise the veil behind which is hidden our destiny after death.

I am sending you by the same mail a lecture which I gave recently at the Académie Delphinale, which is composed of the distinguished men of my province, in which psychical science is almost unknown. Next Friday I shall give another upon your experiences with Miller, and I think I shall have to struggle vigorously against the scepticism of my hearers.

It is because I am well acquainted with the character of our French official scientists, among whom I have spent the greater portion of my life, that I fear I shall not be able to gain all the results you hope from my journey to California. I should have vainly accumulated proofs of the authenticity of the phenomena which I should have witnessed; people will always be inclined to tell me that it is impossible, and that I have allowed myself to be deceived.

You see what happened to Crookes and Dr. Gibier; the latter obtained at General Noël's in Algiers very remarkable materializations, but the majority of those who consent to read the descriptions of them, shrug their shoulders because the committee before which they were shown is composed of persons who are unknown and presided over by a woman.

In my opinion, if we wish to succeed—not in imposing the spirit theory at once, but in showing the materialists that facts contradict their teachings—we must act as I did with Eusapia:

Assemble ten persons who have a well-established scientific reputation;

Request them to settle with me for three or four weeks in any city in France where they could devote themselves exclusively to the study of Miller;

Require of them a collective official report of the seances, with their signatures.

I am almost sure of the adherence of Professors Richet, Flammarion, Porro (Professor of Astronomy in the University of Genoa), of Dr. le Bon (the discoverer of the black light), of Professor Sabathier (dean of the faculty of sciences and author of famous researches in electricity), of Comte de Gramont and Baron de Watteville, both doctors of science, of Maxwell (Attorney-General in Bordeaux), of Colonel Thomassin, grand cross of the legion of honor, of Delanne, etc.

A document signed by these gentlemen would have, not a tenfold, but a hundredfold greater value than a similar one signed by myself alone. As for the very just objection, on the point of the subject's loss of force in a new environment, it may be remedied by sending Miller to me for a fortnight before the commencement of the seances, that he may live with me, and become accustomed to feel confidence in my protection. As to the place where the seances should be held, I will propose several from which to choose, in order to satisfy in the best manner possible the convenience of the members of the committee:

Montpelier, a large and beautiful city, where our senior in age, M. Sabathier, resides.

Bordeaux, where M. Maxwell would facilitate matters for us.

Grenoble, whose environs offer interesting excursions in the intervals of the seances.

Le Vesinet, close by Paris, where one of my friends would offer us the hospitality of his villa for the seances, and where I should live with Miller. To sum up, Monsieur le Professeur, I cannot at this moment accept your generous propositions, but I place myself at your entire disposal to organize in France, at whatever time may best suit your convenience, the experiences with Miller under the conditions which I consider the most favourable to act upon the opinion of my fellow-countrymen.

Please accept, Monsieur le Professeur, the assurance of my highest esteem.

A. DE ROCHAS.

Although these kind words from Count de Rochas d'Aiglun, promising so much for the future, afforded me the greatest pleasure, I nevertheless regret, on account of the cause, that he could not accept my invitation to come here. I hoped that, if a de Rochas could have publicly answered for the extraordinary phenomena which I had observed with Miller, occultism everywhere would have materially benefited.

IV.

As has already been mentioned, the Pacific ocean is about three-quarters of an hour's ride from Los Angeles. From Port Los Angeles to San Pedro—the two extreme northern and southern points—are various watering-places. Santa Monica, Redondo, Long Beach, Playa del Rey, Ocean Park, all more or less primitive; if one finds fault, the American answers: "What do you expect? California is a new country," in which he is certainly correct. The best place is Ocean Park, of course neither an Ostend nor a Nice! Yesterday, April 24, I went by electric car through fields of grain ready for harvesting, past Hollywood, a French colony, and along the spurs of the Sierra Madre of Southern California to Ocean Park to enjoy the sea air and the magnificent flowers, which extend directly to the ocean. Here I fed the pelicans, which, with the sea-gulls, people the ocean and reminded me of Egypt. A sign on a cottage by the shore attracted me: "Madge," the Romany Gypsy Queen, palmist and clairvoyant and crystal-gazer. The latter particularly interested me. Palmists and clairvoyants, of whom in this country there are several in every city, I had visited by dozens, and found three-quarters of them ignorant people, who had drawn their wisdom from worthless books; but every visit costs a dollar, and they often earn an immense amount of money, for the otherwise "smart" American is superstitious. Extremes meet.

Privy Councillor Goldberger is perfectly right when he characterized America as "The Land of Unlimited Possibilities." Every medium here, however, must pay a "license" of thirty dollars monthly. I do not know how it is in the other states of America, but only under these conditions can mediums pursue their business—for that it is here—in California. In Germany, they always stand with one foot in jail.

In France, in 1895, the "Committee for the Defence of the Professional and Scientific Interests of Spiritualism" addressed a full memorial to the Chamber of Deputies, praying for the abrogation of paragraph 7 of article 479 of the "Code pénal" (Penal Code) of February 20, 1810, which prohibits predicting the future and similar things, and for the introduction of a license for the official sanction of this honourable profession. What resulted from it, I do not know.

A crystal-gazer was something new to me; I knew of the existence of such people from occult literature,* but up to this time I had had no personal experiences in this province. Mrs. M. Ingalls—this is her real name—placed a flat crystal cube with octagonal cutting, "a Chinese" one, she said, upon the palm of my left hand, which it nearly covered, and then told me actually almost my entire life. I was not a little surprised. She saw, so she explained this gazing, symbolically in this cube pictures come and go, whose interpretation was the outcome of her experience. The first thing she saw was medical instruments and her first statement was that I must be a physician. True, I was not in the ordinary sense, but for nearly twelve years I made cures with excellent success. She then,

---

*Dr. du Prel's brilliant pen has described this phase of occultism in an extremely interesting way in his romance, *Das Kreuz am Ferner*, Stuttgart, Cotta, 1891, 3d edition, 1905.

with wonderful accuracy, told me my thoughts, my character, my disappointments, and my struggles;* all this in a little cottage, directly on the shore of the great ocean, whose waves almost washed the walls of the little wooden house. Somnambulists and crystal-gazers seem to be able to state past and coming events most accurately; materialized phantoms can do this less positively, since they are obliged to take too much from the medium himself, hence absolutely genuine communications can scarcely be expected from them.

Here I am now sitting in the arbour in my garden while describing my yesterday's experiences. For nearly three years I have seen neither snow nor ice except on the mountain peaks of the Sierra Nevada, which are distinctly in view from this spot, for this is the region of perpetual sunshine and summer; overcoats are almost unknown, and my furs lie buried in naphthaline to protect them against

---

*To suffer oneself, in order to present proofs, will ever remain the most beautiful and fruitful anthropomorphism. It makes us ethical and gives us strength. Ernst von Feuchtersleben: *Zur Diätetik der Seele* (Dietetics of the Soul). I have often heard similar statements from spiritual beings, who alleged that they were my guides.

moths, packed in strong chests. The ice-sports of Berlin's "Rousseau Island" are totally unknown here. Eleven palm-trees of different kinds stand in my garden, among orange, lemon, peach, banana, and fig trees, which latter produce black figs almost as large as my hand. The lemon trees are already bearing new blossoms, although the old fruit is not yet fully ripe. The magnificent bougainvillea, with its thousands of lilac blossoms and the yellow bigonia are twining up to the roof of my house, and in the so-called winter season. The *Deutsche Zeitung* of April 7, received to-day—the mail is from eighteen to twenty-two days in reaching here—reports zero weather and snow in Berlin. While reading this, I do not feel much longing for the low-lying plains of North Germany.

In my opinion the United States has a tolerably large dark side in their temperance movement. I am no drinker, though I do not at all despise a glass of wine, but what the temperance people have accomplished here is almost incomprehensible to German ideas. In the states of Maine, Iowa, Kansas, North Dakota, the sale of alcohol is prohibited. Now in Los Angeles beer can be had only when a whole meal is ordered. And what beer! Germans would refuse it. In social gatherings one almost always receives only ice-water at lunch or dinner. In the Luxor Hotel, at Luxor, in Egypt, I witnessed for the first time this sight, which is positively comical to Germans.

At dinner there a party of Americans sat at a long table at the right, and at the left a party of Germans. Before each plate of the Germans stood a bottle of wine, before each one of the Americans a glass of ice-water. In spite of this, the American drinks, when he does drink, more than the German. Yet one constantly reads of suicides as the result of the effects of alcoholism. Like the beverages, all eatables are three or four times as dear as in Germany, and whoever perhaps is accustomed to Dressel and Hiller in Berlin, the "Maison Dorée" in Paris, the Savoy Hotel in London, must greatly reduce his demands here. Except turkey with cranberry sauce—the American national dish—and mutton chops a gastronomist will not find much to enjoy, unless he is satisfied with fruit, which in California certainly leaves nothing to be desired.

The Indian "Vedanta Society" has established a mission here, as well as in San Francisco, a mission which has a very agreeable representative and teacher in Mr. Swami Sachchidananda. I am not competent to give an opinion of the esoteric doctrine of Buddhism and the Vedanta system. Sinnett* did not interest me, which is of course no argument against the eventual truth of the Indian theosophy. The devout Indian does not fear death, but an unfavourable reincarnation. The world offers him nothing which would be to him worth gaining, worth enjoying, or worth knowing, except Brahma.†

This is not the place to discuss the value of this doctrine, and I am besides too much of a layman to be able to form a trustworthy opinion, but I received the impression: all this can be, but perhaps it cannot be.

Evidently the matter in question here deals with intuitive perceptions, that is purely theoretical conclusion, which can offer no assurance. The modern age of physical science wishes to be convinced by experiments, and

---

*A. P. Sinnett: *Esoteric Buddhism.*
†See also *Three Lectures on the Vedanta Philosophy,* by Max Müller, London: Longmans, Green & Co., 1894.

therefore, though theosophy may look down scornfully upon Spiritualistic essays, I am firmly convinced that it alone will gradually lead science, by experimental paths, to the perception that there is a spirit which survives the earthly husk. The cosmogony of an A. J. Davis,* and Hudson Tuttle† is far more sympathetic to me than the theory of evolution, which Sinnett publishes as revelations of Indian theosophy, though, for the rest, a chapter from the Gospels, whose meaning becomes clearer through the experiences of modern occultism than orthodoxy understands how to make it, personally affords me far more pleasure than the rationalism of a Davis, whose *Philosophy of Death*‡ is considered the best thing which the revelations of Spiritualism has ever published.

So far as I have understood the previously mentioned Indian, he preaches a sort of pantheism in the meaning of Spinoza, combined with mystic ideas, such as we find in Xeno-

---

*A. J. Davis: *The Principles of Nature.*
†Hudson Tuttle: *History and Laws of the Events of Creation;* also *Philosophy of the Spirit and the Spirit World.*
‡A. J. Davis: *The Physician.*

phanes, Plato, Eckart, Theophrastus Paracelsus, Giordano Bruno, Böhme, and others.

But at any rate the assertion, which the noble Annie Besant also upholds, that suicides and persons who are suddenly deprived of life by accident would be worse off in the World Beyond,* if they did not have a pure and good life behind them, is extremely open to dispute. My own practical experience, and those of others, for instance with astrology, which I studied through its best representatives, as George Wilde and Alan Leo in England, and especially Albert Kniepf in Hamburg, point much more to an absolute destination of human destiny. That chiromancy and somnambulism often accurately predict for us future events, I consider as established facts. I remember Mme. de Thèbes† in Paris, the Berlin prophetess de Ferriëm, the testimonials for the predictions of Cazotte by Laharpe,‡ and hundreds of other examples to be found in spiritualistic literature.

---

*Annie Besant: *Ueber Mediumismus* (Concerning Mediums), Sphinx, 1894, p. 380.

†*Psychical Studies*, 1896, p. 467; 1897, pp. 198, 647, etc.

‡*Psychical Studies*, 1898, p. 455, by Dr. Walter Bormann. See Bulwer's *Zanoni*, Leipsic, 1842, p. 72.

An Occultist's Travels. 87

According to these, there are destinies which cannot be changed; so why should a person who was deprived of life by a so-called accident, which he could not foresee, be obliged to atone so heavily for it? The present editor of *Psychical Studies,* Professor Maier, as well as Privy Councillor Seiling, have at times expressed themselves on the justification of suicide, under certain conditions,* in a sense to which the majority of readers probably would find little to object. If my predestination will permit, I shall, however, soon visit India, in order, if possible, to study the "esoteric doctrine" at the source.

With the very influential position of woman in America, where she stands infinitely higher than in Europe, the Indian theosophy—the Vedanta system is certainly one of the principal ones—ought certainly to have little success, when the American woman hears the opinion of Buddha concerning the female sex. It is similar to Schopenhauer's and Nietzsche's! Dr. Max Freiherr von Wimpffen† writes the fol-

---

*See *Psychical Studies,* 1900, p. 489, and 1901, p. 165.
†*Kritische Worte über den Buddhismus* (Critical Words on Buddhism), Vienna, Carl Konegen, 1891. See Hermann Oldenberg: *Buddah, sein leben, sein*

lowing: "The Enlightened One has a strange opinion of the weaker sex. Every woman will commit a sin, if she has the opportunity or finds a suitable place or a convenient tempter, if necessary with a cripple, if no one better is at hand. Unfathomably concealed, like the pathway of the fish in the water, is the nature of woman, the shrewd robber, in whom truth is hard to find, to whom falsehood is like truth and truth like falsehood," etc.

Occult monism, as principally represented by Hellenbach and du Prel, satisfies the needs of the human mind and soul in a totally different way from the Indian theosophy; this was always my impression, which my experiences, though insignificant, confirmed.

The boundary which separates the two worlds (the spiritual and the material) may gradually fall, like many other barriers, and we shall attain a higher comprehension of the unity of Nature. The number of the possible things in the universe is as great as its extent. What we

---

Lehre, seine Gemeinde (Buddha, his Life, his Doctrine, his Community), Berlin, 1881, and Heinrich Kern: *Der Buddhismus und seine Geschichte in Indien* (Buddhism and its History in India), translated by Hermann Jacobi, Leipzig, 1882.

know is nothing in comparison with that which still remains for us to know. *If we were willing to satisfy ourselves with the half-possession, which we have hitherto attained, we should be traitors to the holiest rights of science!*

Since writing the above, I have come across the following article in the *Progressive Thinker* (Chicago, Sept. 28, 1907), in which the doctrine of reincarnation is clearly and forcibly stated:

"Having been a careful reader of *The Progressive Thinker* for more than three years past, I have noted with pleasure its numerous contributed brilliant articles from the great thinkers of the day.

"But I have also wondered, not a little at some of the curious conceptions regarding reincarnation, which are therein occasionally expressed by the army of inquirers, scoffers, or skeptics, who in many instances have confessedly investigated little, and flung their speculations broadcast from quite insufficiently gathered knowledge concerning these great teachings. It is true that those who have not awakened to the truth of rebirth cannot have it forced upon them by argument, while those to whom it appeals do not need the argument. Yet there are many by whom it is vaguely felt to be true teaching, who yet fail to grasp its significance, being, indeed, repelled by its seeming incongruities. To such in the fullness of time come illumination, not argument. The teaching is often revealed through unexpected sources and comes in humble guise.

"For the present writer the mystery called reincarnation came as a revelation, certain facts being explainable on no other hypothesis.

"The doctrine of compulsory rebirth; that man is bound to the wheel of repeated incarnations, and into lower forms is justly repugnant to the mind which holds sacred the eternal justice of things. Such is not the teaching.

"Man is reborn strictly with his own consent and desire, and continuance of consciousness—*the consciousness depending upon the degree of spiritual attainment acquired by the soul in its development up through numerous existences.*

"When a soul has accumulated to itself the varied experiences of an earth life, it passes on into the plane prepared by its own measure of progress, there to remain not "through centuries of oblivion," but in conscious enjoyment and assimilation of the same experiences gathered during its late incarnation. Sooner or later, however, according to the degree of development, the soul, resting in exalted happiness, having assimilated all its earth experience, and in obedience to some latent, unfulfilled desire, seeks earthly experience again.

"The desire is prophecy of its own fulfillment—desire and will are back of the evolutionary urge from the beginning of unfoldment.

"But the developed soul gains this at last, through repeated incarnations; he has awakened to a knowledge, and henceforth waits on the higher planes, until such time as the earth and race progress have swung round to a point where he can reincarnate with advantage to his desire fulfillment.

It sometimes happens that the desire of the incarnating soul is opposed by the superior wisdom of the Spirit, knowing always what is best, and the result is an earth life—like many which we know, of noble, struggling souls—torn by conflict and contradiction. Yet still is 'all well' for its unfailing guide, the true Ego, will inevitably lead toward the absolute in ultimate perfection.

"In the case of the undeveloped soul, they, having little spirituality, reincarnate more frequently, retaining no memories whatever of any previous existence, because these must be intuitive, and being brought back to earth by force of attraction and blind desire.

"But each time they gain some slight advance. Never a retrogression is made. The earth is a school and its vacations are meant to be spent in happy recreations. One may spend hundreds of years in the same grade, but eventually it is mastered, and they pass into the next highest. Should a scholar fail in only one study, he is sent back to be made perfect in that one. The other studies of his class, having been learned, are his own acquired property, and cannot be taken from him. Thus does the soul gain, if it be but a few strands which are woven into the pattern all must shape for eternity.

"It is strictly upon the plane of its own making that the higher spirit enjoys larger periods of repose and beatitude, while the lower spirit comes more quickly back to earth life from which he is indeed but severed by the casting off of the fleshly garment. The fact of the lower entities more quickly reincarnating, while the higher are in a state of conscious waiting for more suitable earth conditions, furnishes a key to the mystery of the rise and fall of nations, the ebb and flow of great dynasties, and the thinking mind gains historical events which have been chronicled in the world's records since time began for us.

"The separation of loved ones by reincarnation, so often loudly lamented, is no more brought about than is the case in any other temporary remorse on the earth-plane. The law of attraction holds good in all cases, and those who have been brought together into close relations by a present incarnation, had previously established conditions operating under its law in past lives. It sometimes happens, however, that a soul on the higher planes may wait centuries, while the soul of some loved one, less developed, must return for other experiences and lessons and also in obedience to latent desire, while the higher soul is consciously watching and waiting for the one dear to it though less advanced in spiritual progress. Does this seem hard and long? Then please remember that in the vast scheme of eternity a thousand years are but a day, and a day a thousand years; and, look you, what happens!

"When, according to the inevitable working of the law of attraction, these two souls meet again, they take up their lives together and henceforward are never more separated.

"They have reached the planes of true wisdom and unfoldment and are 'saved' from further re-birth on the earth-plane. Hereafter it is on the spiritual zones that they continually progress, or else voluntarily return, as did the great teachers, to help on in the development of the whole race.

"Thus, when the soul through right living, which is loving, has reached these heights, there is for it then no more re-births in blind obedience to latent desire. It has awakened to the light of truth, and henceforward comes understandingly, if at all.

"In the minds of many are clear revelations of former lives. Friendships discovered, loves reunited after centuries of Karmic severance; destinies worked out to complete fulfillment through ages of preparation—thus does the soul come into its inheritance, and is illumined for eternity.

"These beliefs have existed in the minds of millions since the world began. We cannot think of anything which can transcend the universe of thought, hence it must be possible, and if possible, one can see how, to those millions of people, it has become demonstrable truth. And, after all, it is a beautiful and consoling thing, once faced, and its seeming incongruities assimilated; this doctrine of reincarnation; spiritual evolution, and a growth into eternity from germ to God!

"Again, there have been those who speak of the soul as 'dwarfing' back to infancy when it reincarnates. The spirit, in or out of incarnation, is in full identity. Can we not conceive of one trying a boat, little by little, step by step, ere he seizes the oars and pulls out into the full stream? So the spirit watches over its own and bides its time for fullness of manifestation. The selfhood can and does come and go, and waits upon its tools of mind and brain until it is able to step in and assume command intelligently; using them and testing them until they respond, at last, in fullness of maturity, to the soul's need of expression.

"And the mother need not fear that she is

singing her lullaby to a monster or cynic philosopher, full-fledged, who scoffs, through his meal of milk at the inadequacy of his environments; she is nursing her 'bud of humanity' which has existed, indeed, since a spark, it sprang, back in the eons of time, from the bosom of flame, but for her it is a waiting, dreaming soul, which has selected and been selected into this same environment through the aid of spirit, in obedience to the very law of attraction which brought the two together in the past, loving and beloved.

"Many say they do not want to live again; certainly not, not the same life; but a new life is a continuation, not a repetition. Personalities pass; individuals remain unchanged save as they are built into by the character structure which perfects the true and eternal ego. The new life marks but another chapter in the great Human book.

"As to Karma, we know that as we sow so must we reap. Regarding the aid and sympathy we must render to our brother, struggling in the meshes wrought by his own acts, see to it that we judge not, neither withhold. That is our part, if we are progressing spiritually.

"By these acts of mercy and love are we

destined to mitigate the Karma of some suffering soul which is thus brought into touch with heavenly ministrations, and gradually released from the operations of the law. The child is burned by putting its hand into the fire.

"Cause and effect follow one another with unerring accuracy, but woe be to the one who stands aside through misunderstanding of the Karmic law, and withholds the kindly oil which shall alleviate its pain! New Karmic conditions, and a disastrous chain of cause and effect would thus be established, reacting upon the one who shall judge his brother, withholding sympathy and help! Doing so, we are involved in our own acts, and the conditions which they create. These we have begotten; with our brother's we have naught to do, save to love him and help him. We do not necessarily reincarnate in order that we may commit all of the sins (ignorances) which we are in the midst of here; but if we fail in help or sympathy with our brother who has fallen into the mire, then shall we be brought into such personal relation with those same evils that we shall learn, through experience, to be merciful, understanding, and to judge not.

"After all, reincarnation means but a Day from Home! Heaven is Home! The labourer goes forth to return at nightfall. Earth is more than a starting-point. Its seed-times and harvest are wrought out here. But the Eternal Harvest is the rendering unto God of the accumulated talents of many lives, which as captains of industry we have faithfully garnered up through the ages of probation and trial here. This makes it imperative that we live well and royally, and to live well, is to *Love Much*.

"LAURA FITZHUGH PRESTON.
"Fernandina, Fla."

V.

My desire to see ice and snow again, and once more be able to shiver, was fulfilled more quickly than I anticipated. The Pacific Coast Steamship Co., whose ships run from San Diego, on the Mexican frontier, to Alaska, arranges in summer several excursions from Tacoma in Washington to Alaska, and so I immediately joined the first one, which left Tacoma on the 8th of June. From Los Angeles to this place is a journey of sixty hours by rail, before reaching the steamer. I again passed, as in 1904, the snow-clad Mount Shasta, 14,450 feet high, with its famous Shasta springs, then Portland in Oregon, where the Exposition was being held, and at last reached Tacoma, which, surrounded by mountains, is magnificently situated on the water, from which Mt. Rainier, completely covered with snow, rises to the height of 14,440 feet. Here, with perhaps one hundred and fifty passengers, I went on board the steamer "Spokane." Our first landing was at Seattle, the second Port Victoria at Vancouver, which belongs to British Columbia, Canada, then we went forty-two hours northward between the island of Vancouver and the continent of British Columbia, till, as the first stopping-place we reached Ketchikan in Alaska, where our ship was received by a band of Indians with music. The United States purchased Alaska in 1867 for $7,200,000. The House of Representatives in Washington opposed the purchase, as many of them thought it valueless. To-day Alaska produces about $30,000,000 in gold annually, aside from the great wealth in fisheries. Russia might, therefore, greatly regret having sold Alaska. Alaska has the greatest gold stamp-mill in the world, the "Treadwell mine," whose owners are said to be the London Rothschilds. The journey was beautiful everywhere; as soon as we approached the Taku glacier, which rises from the sea between two mountain peaks and is about half a mile wide and two hundred feet high, blocks of ice in the strangest forms, blue as sapphire, came floating toward us. A wonderful spectacle! The most northern point which we reached was

Skagway and the White Pass, which travellers must traverse to reach the Klondike gold fields. An icy chill came to us from the Muir glacier, and our ship slowly ploughed her way through the ice-sea of Glacier Bay. On the heights of Killisnoo, on Admiralty Island, we fished with excellent success; a sixty-pound halibut was the largest catch.

In Sitka, too, the capital of Alaska, on Baranof Island, we stopped and saw the Greek church which the Russians left there; true, it is not the Kremlin in Moscow, which I visited in 1887, but it possesses several oil paintings which one would not have expected to see in this forsaken country. The inhabitants of this region are the Alaska Indians, but they are tolerably civilized. One still sees many "totem poles," the idols carved from the trunk of a tree by these Indians; but the United States has done a great deal here and established missions everywhere. It was broad daylight until eleven o'clock at night, and the sun rose again at two o'clock in the morning. This excursion lasted eleven days; we reached Seattle again on the 19th of June, 1905.

I have now visited the principal objects of interest in the United States except Niagara, which I unfortunately passed at night, and can sum up my opinion as follows: "The Yosemite is beautiful; the Yellowstone is wonderful; the Grand Cañon of Arizona is colossal, and Alaska, with its fjords and mountains, glaciers, and rivers, possibilities and distances, is all of these. It is not only colossal, but wonderful and beautiful as well."

On the way back from Tacoma I again spent several days in San Francisco, to see Miller and learn whether he would now be ready to go with me to de Rochas in France. But business matters prevented his doing so at present; he promised, however, to accompany me to France in April, 1906, which I informed de Rochas. His answer, dated Château de l'Agnélas, near Voiron, June 20, 1905, expressed his pleasure at my intelligence. I hope I shall succeed in taking Miller to France next spring.

I will describe a few more seances which produced something new. In one which took place May 25, 1905, a white ball like muslin again sank from the ceiling before the curtain with a swinging movement to the floor, then rolled to my seat, upward along my left leg, *against every natural law,* pressed closely to my heart, rolled down again upon the floor, directly at my feet, where it quickly developed as a spirit and told me that she was Jemima Clark (an English medium) and had made the attempt to connect herself with my magnetism, which was usually too fiery for such experiments: yet she had succeeded, and hoped that I was pleased, which I willingly admitted.

This is the same spirit, who in the test seance at the Palace Hotel produced the best phenomena, next to Betsy, the main control. The following experiment was also interesting: Betsy appeared before the curtain with Miller whom she requested to bring the lamp, which stood about twenty-three feet away, so that we saw her, for about three minutes, fully illuminated, after which she sank down.* A former patient, the widow of a Grand Duke of a South German reigning House, who had died about eight weeks before, also came, embraced me with great delight, gave her full name, and showed the same mannerisms, which I had often noticed in her in life. To *prove* an identity, as is

---

*See Aksakov: *Animismus und Spiritismus* (Animism and Spiritualism), Leipsic, Oswald Mutze, 1894, **I, p.** 240, and Florence Marryat: *There is no Death.*

well known to one familiar with occultism, is the most difficult thing in such cases. A short time after death it is more possible; but when the spirit has progressed farther in its development, that is, has especially developed the principle of love, it has, according to my experience, to struggle to forget the mire of earth more and more in order to progress, and then the identity is difficult to prove, because the *personality* has vanished, and only the *individuality* has remained, which, however, usually has to develop in a totally different direction from what the sphere of earth permits.

I also attended a "trumpet sitting." I heard the trumpets flying about in all the corners of the room, heard voices speak through them, saw everywhere little flames from which words were spoken; but as the room, meanwhile, was kept perfectly dark, I will not describe this seance as at all conclusive. In another seance Betsy told me that she would show me, for once, what often happened in seances with other materialization mediums, that is, that frequently the medium himself, disguised as a spirit, appeared, the term for it was "impersonation." She asked me to come directly to the curtain and told me that the medium, in a trance, would come out in white muslin, and the muslin would then suddenly disappear; and so it was! I grasped the medium, who had come out of the cabinet disguised as a spirit, by the hand. Like a flash of lightning the white veiling vanished, and I clasped the medium with my hand.

In all these seances Miller, if he was in the cabinet, and I saw the phantoms myself without him, was obliged to clap his hands continually, in order to silence my doubt whether the phantom might perhaps be a transfiguration. Kiesewetter* writes concerning this: "Here it is only suggested that there is a kind of pseudo-materialization, in which the medium, lying in hypnosis, walks in a somnambulistic condition, playing the part of spirit, wherein the mysterious vanishing of the spiritual veilings point to a commencing magical activity of the psychic.

After having previously called attention to the relative value of spiritual communications, I have no reason to quote them, for the reader now knows that *they are to be taken critically.*

---

*Karl Kiesewetter: *Geschichte des neueren Okkultismus* (History of Modern Occultism), Leipzig, Wilhelm Friedrich, p. 607.

For instance, this time an unhappy spirit—the control Betsy said she had been too much occupied to be able to prevent it—stole into his seances. It was a female black spirit, that went about the circle of fourteen persons, striking and spitting upon nearly all of them, and continually using abusive language. She touched me on the left leg and said in English: "You want to go to Europe with this medium—I'll fix you" (that is, I'll prevent the manifestations!). Betsy told me afterward that this spirit had given a minister of the Episcopal church two hundred thousand dollars, because he had promised her that, after her death, she should see Christ. As this had not followed, she was so furious that she injured Spiritualism wherever she could. Whole companies of Jesuit spirits were doing the same, and in Europe Spiritualism would have advanced much farther, if such spirits, whose influences and thoughts hung like a wall over Europe, did not so eagerly oppose Spiritualism."* *"The church does not want to lose her power."* The church does not want to lose the stream of millions

---

*See Dr. Friese: *Stimmen aus dem Reich der Geister* (Voices from the Realm of Spirits), Leipzig, Oswald Mutze, 1897, p. 92.

which, under the name of Peter's Pence, is annually directed to Rome, and happiness in the world beyond the grave is made dependent upon the means of grace of the church. Christ's successor has become a bank director in the Vatican. It is no longer: "Feed my lambs! but shear my sheep!"*

In the year 1887 I visited the Vatican in Rome, and now understood the power of the Catholic Church. The vast magnificence of the Vatican, as well as that of the church of St. Mark in Venice, in which I heard a Te Deum with trombones, which penetrated the very depths of my being, and the Kremlin in Moscow, exert in themselves a very powerful impression upon the ordinary man, which is increased by the processions, and which even I myself, though a Protestant, was unable to escape.

In San Francisco I also had an opportunity to meet a second crystal-gazer, who was recommended to me by friends. Her name is Mlle. M. Wille, 310 Ellis Street. She was not inferior to Mrs. Ingalls in Ocean Park, of whom

---

*Dr. du Prel: *Der Tod,* etc. (Death, etc.), p. 111 and following.

I have already spoken; only her crystal consisted of a glass ball as large as an ordinary marble. She saw in this glass ball, after I had held it in my hand three minutes, in pictures, precisely like Mrs. Ingalls, all the principal events of my life.

On the journey to Alaska I had taken for reading *Parerga and Paralipomena* by Schopenhauer, in which I found the following assertion: "Neither our *actions nor our career in life* is our own work, but probably that which no one thinks of our *character and existence.* For, on the basis of these, and the circumstances and external events occurring in the strictest causal connection, our acts and life career move forward with absolute necessity. Therefore, at the birth of man, his whole course of life, down to the details, is irrevocably appointed, so that a somnambulist of the highest power could predict it exactly. We ought to keep in mind this great and absolute truth in the consideration and judgment of our course in life, our acts, and our sorrows."

"I teach," so Dr. du Prel sums up the meaning of his system built upon the perception"— that man has entered the earthly life of his own choice; that he is the product of his own development; that man ought to address to himself all the charges with which he loads God, Destiny, and Nature; that the sufferings of this life result in the transcendental benefit of our character."*

A. J. Davis † also positively denies free will in the words "The doctrine of the free will or action of the soul is positively contradicted by everything in nature and in mankind," which assertion he then pursues in detail. Baron Hellenbach expresses himself as follows: "We have perceived that freedom of will in the phenomenal world is only apparent, and is one of the prejudices of the ordinary mind, in the same way as our personality and all nature, whose real foundation and factors lie in a supersensible world."

Hellenbach has also expressed himself elsewhere in detail about the apparent liberty of

---

*Du Prel draws this belief from the pre-existence of transcendental subjects, in which he assumes that the act of will directed to re-incarnation coincides with the procreative impulse of the parents.
†A. J. Davis: *The Teacher.*
‡L. B. Hellenbach: *Die Vorurtheile der Menschheit* (The Prejudices of Mankind), Leipzig, Mutze, II, p. 92. See also his little known, but important work, *Die Magie der Zahlen* (The Magic of Numbers), the same.

the will. My own experience with somnambulists and mediums who possessed the gift of looking into the future is, that man has a compulsory itinerary, which he cannot alter, and which brings him, for the most part, trials to develop his character. His duty is to accept them in humility, according to Christ's example and relying upon Christ's word. For instance, Christ was to be betrayed, and the temptation to do so came to Judas; the latter might not have wanted to do it—that was his sin—but then it would have been done by some other representative of the species "man"!

The earthly life is to the majority of mankind a vale of tears, but even a period of eighty years is only like a dream of the night in comparison with eternity, and he who has not learned to know misfortune does not know how to value the happiness which the next existence offers—this is the quintessence of all the wisdom of life.

"The necessity of our acts seems to take from us the responsibility for them, and yet almost every one, if he rises even a small degree above the brute, feels that this is not so. His satisfaction or dissatisfaction, after a deed is done, speaks loudly against it; every one feels that he really ought to act in this way or that. There is no doubt about the 'Thou shalt' existing within us; even the criminal feels under certain circumstances that he has done something which he ought not to have done. From this 'ought' has arisen the belief in the freedom of the will; we have seen that this is only apparent, and yet we feel the responsibility—not for our acts, but for our being."*

Schopenhauer, too, has raised no barrier against responsibility; he believes with Kant that liberty can be reconciled with empirical necessity; he says: Man, it is true, cannot act otherwise than according to his nature; but he might be different; therefore the responsibility does not concern the deed, but always the character of the doer. The expression, "I am ashamed of having done such a thing," is a prejudice of the ordinary mind, and ought to run, "I am ashamed of my nature in being able or compelled to do such a thing; I ought to have done—that is, to have been—otherwise."

Dr. du Prel's mode of explanation, that the

---

*Hellenbach: *Die Vorurtheile der Menschheit* (The Prejudices of Mankind), II, p. 90.

transcendental subject was the organizing principle in us, so that we ourselves were the architects of our earthly lives, making the doctrines of Schopenhauer and Hellenbach still more intelligible.*

Very beautiful are the words of the poem which the medium, Princess Mary Karadja, has written under inspiration, for which reason I append them here:

"Man may not cross the plans of the Most High;
It is not for him to decide on death or life.
The lessons of the earthly life he *must* learn;
He is not permitted to leave it at his pleasure.
The body is a garment that is laid aside,
When the soul has grown beyond its worn-out shroud,
And has become mature for transformation."†

In the same meaning, Goethe says:

"And so, once more, 'tis as the planets would;
  Conditions, limits, laws, our fate decide;

---

*The Philosophy of Mysticism, New York: *The Path*, 144 Madison ave., $7.50.
†Mary Karadja: *Zum Licht* (To the Light), Leipzig, Max Spohr, 1900.

We will the right, because we see we should;
  And thus by our own hands our wills are tied.
The heart drives out its hopes, a much-loved brood;
  At the stern must wishes and whims subside,
So, after many years in seeming free,
More closely fettered than at first are we."*

   (Translation by James Freeman Clarke.)

To-day, July 18, 1905, I received the July number of *Psychical Studies,* in which I read that Professor Charles Richet† has proposed the expression, "Metapsychics," for the whole province of investigation which is usually termed "Occult Science." As this designation seems to me, as well as to the editor of *Psychical Studies,* to be very happily chosen, I shall henceforth employ it.

Here in Los Angeles, as occurs every year, a Spiritualist camp was established in Mineral Park from the 25th of June to the 25th of

---

   *Goethe: *Necessity* in *Gott und Welt* (God and the World), Leipzig (Bibl. Institut.), I, p. 324.
   †Ludwig Deinhard: *Der 5 Internationale Psychologen-Kongress in Rom* (The 5th International Psychological Congress in Rome), *Psychical Studies,* 1905, p. 405.

July, 1905. About a dozen mediums of all phases had met there, but not a single one could be used. Such pseudo-mediums do more harm than good, since they chatter the most absurd nonsense. In Germany, such a thing would not be possible. The police would soon put a check on this sort of liberty, which, it is true, is acting without judgment, as brutal force never ripens good fruit. Genuine and good mediums are rare, and governments ought rather to appoint trained experts for the investigation of the phenomena and the testing of real mediums; but when shall we—especially in Germany—progress so far? Yesterday (August 1) I visited by recommendation a young lady, who calls herself "Cleo," Psychist and Clairvoyant, and lives at 210 Mercantile Place. She speaks English and also German, but the latter not fluently, though she said she was born in Emden (East Friesland). She requested me to write six questions, with my name and day of birth, and give them to her in a closed envelope; I did this in another room and then handed her the closed envelope. She took it in her hand, and told me fluently my questions in succession and my name! This Cleo would easily have earned the "prix Burdin" of 3000 francs* which Professor Ludwig Büchner and Professor C. Mendel wrongly believe will never be earned by a clairvoyant. Du Prel has answered the misrepresentation of the original facts on the part of Dr. Mendel in a way† which is really excellent. One really ought not to believe that a physician of such reputation as Professor Mendel could put forth into the world so pitiable an essay. Cleo proved to me absolutely, with regard to the past, that she possesses the gift of clairvoyance; whether her predictions concerning my future will be correct is to be determined; at any rate, I was glad to hear that I need remain only four or five years longer upon this earth. I hope she is not mistaken! I feel like Thomas Hobbes, who, when his physician, on the 4th of December, 1679, in reply to his question whether he might

---

*Dr. Pigeaire: *Pruissance de l'electricite animale* (Power of Animal Electricity), Paris, 1839, pp. 116-118; Dr. Frappart, *Lettres sur le magnétisme et le somnambulisme à l'occasion de Mademoiselle Pigeaire* (Letters upon magnetism and somnambulism in reference to Miss Pigeaire), p. 23.

†*Professor Dr. C. Mendel in Berlin und der Hypnotismus* (Professor Dr. C. Mendel in Berlin and Hypnotism), by Dr. Med. and Phil. Carl Gerster and Dr. Phil. Carl du Prel, Leipzig, William Friedrich, 1890.

expect to live, answered in the negative, said to him: "Well, then, I will rejoice to find a hole through which I can creep out of this world."

Du Prel,* too, is of the same opinion, when he writes: "When we by the benefit of death, have recovered from the earthly life and awake to the life in the world beyond, we shall say, like the dying Socrates to his friend Krito: 'We must sacrifice a cock to Æsculapius.'"

---

*Du Prel: *Der Tod, das Jenseits, das Leben im Jenseits* (Death, the World Beyond, Life in the World Beyond), Munich, 1899, p. 39.

VI.

Whoever is familiar with the older magnetic literature* will find an enormous quantity of

---

*The most important sources are: Dr. Arnold Wienholt, *Heilkraft des tierischen Magnetismus* (Healing Power of Animal Magnetism), 5 volumes, Lemgo, 1802; Dr. Friedrich Hufeland, *Ueber Sympathie* (Upon Sympathy), Weimar, 1811; Professor C. A. F. Kluge, *Versuch einer Darstellung des animalischen Magnetismus* (Attempt at a Description of Animal Magnetism), Berlin, 1811; *Archiv für tierischen Magnetismus* (Archives of Animal Magnetism), 12 volumes, by Professor Eschenmayer, Professor Kieser, Professor Nasse, Professor Nees von Esenbeck, Altenburg (Brockhaus), 1817-1824; Professor Nees von Esenbeck, *Entwicklungsgeschichte des magnetischen Schlafs und Traums* (History of the Development of the Magnetic Sleep and Dreams), Bonn, 1820; Dupotet, *Elementare Darstellung des tierischen Magnetismus*, Grimma, 1851; Professor J. Ennemoser,*Anleitung zur mesmerischen Praxis* (Guidance in Mesmeric Practice), Stuttgart, 1852; Baron von Reichenbach, *Der sensitive Mensch* (The Sensitive Human Being), Stuttgart, 1854; Dr. George Barth, *Der Lebensmagnetismus* (Magnetism), Heilbronn, 1852; Justinus Kerner, *Die Seherin von Prevorst* (The Seeress of Prevorst), Leipzig, Reclam; Cahagnet, *Der Verkehr mit den Verstorbenen* (Intercourse with the Departed), Hildburghhausen, 1851; Deleuze, *Praktischer Unterricht über den tierischen Magnetismus* (Practical Instruction in Animal Magnetism), Stuttgart, 1854.

analogous examples of clairvoyance. It is only to be regretted that it is difficult to obtain them, since du Prel, usually the best treasure-house of such curiosities, rarely mentions the place of publication and the date when these books appeared.

In the *"Archives of Animal Magnetism"* all this is still to be most conveniently found; but the majority of these works are mouldering in the libraries, and I have spent years in purchasing the principal ones. The libraries of du Prel, Carl Kiesewetter, and Dr. Ed. Reich, the latter which seemed to me particularly valuable, I saw in 1900 during my visit to Scheveningen—ought to be kept together for the general benefit.

It is well known that the history of animal magnetism is a blot upon the history of medicine. It will not be forgotten that there were physicians who drove the talented Mesmer into a dishonorable exile, because he cured the sick without pills; I myself fared little better, though the commission of eleven physicians appointed by the Paris Academy for the investigation of Magnetism and Somnambulism, after five years' investigation, voted unanimously in 1831 for Magnetism, and corroborated all the remarkable phenomena attributed to Somnambulism.*

Professor Ed. Gasc. Desfossés,† who has compiled excellently the latest experiences in the province of magnetism, writes as follows:

"The doctrine of vital magnetism will then have made a long stage, a long scientific novitiate; but it will end, we are firmly convinced, by triumphing, and by finally conquering its legitimate place in science. It must be recognized that very recently a victory of considerable importance has been gained by the idea of magnetism: a decision of the Minister of Public Instruction, dated March 26th, 1895, has classed among the great free higher schools the Practical School of Magnetism and Massage founded by M. Le Professeur H. Durville, and placed under the patronage of the Magnetic Society of France."

True, there are some praiseworthy exceptions among German physicians; for instance, Sur-

---

*Professor Dr. J. Ochorowicz: *Magnetismus und Hypnotismus* (Magnetism and Hypnotism), Leipzig, Oswald Mutze, 1897, p. 75.

†Gasc. Desfossés: *Magnétisme Vital*, Paris (Société d'Editions Scientifiques), 4 Rue Antoine, Dubois, 1897, p. 26.

geon-General von Stuckrad personally expressed to me the following opinion, which I will add in his honor and the interest of the cause:

"After repeated treatment by Professor Willy Reichel, I have reached the conviction that by the direct contact through laying the palms of the hands on various parts of the body there passes from Professor Reichel* to the patients an invigorating, extremely beneficial influence, which may be compared to an agreeable and strengthening current affecting the nervous system; under the palm of the hand a feeling of increased warmth instantly developed in me, and quickly spread, radiating in every direction, whether the application of the hands was on the back laterally from the spine, or in the pit of the stomach, in the region of the heart. The direct effect of the magnetic treatment consisted in the undoubted feeling of warmth, strengthening, and invigoration, combined with the comfort of repeated,

---

*See Willy Reichel: *Healing Magnetism, etc.*, 3d edition, Berlin, 1896, p. 90, and *Journal du Magnétisme* (Journal of Magnetism), 50th year, Paris, 1895, April number.

very deep inspiration. What has hitherto become known to me concerning the efficaciousness of animal magnetism, especially through its obvious success in curing various diseases, leads me to the earnest wish that it might be generally and minutely studied, and find the most extensive application possible in healing institutions of every description; and this wish is fully supported and justified by the literature and practice of many years past, as well as of the present time.

"Dr. von Stuckrad, *Surgeon-General.*
"Berlin, August, 1894."

Dr. du Prel* says: "The accidental circumstance that a physician, Mesmer, discovered animal magnetism, has caused it to be regarded chiefly in its physiological effects, that is, as a branch of therapeutics. But owing to a complication of circumstances, there has been endless strife with official medical science. Through Reichenbach the investigation was transferred to the province of physics, where the proofs are exposed to fewer objections. Summing up the whole, it may be asserted to-day that animal

---

*Du Prel: *Death, the World Beyond, etc.,* Munich.

magnetism is proved (1) by the physiological changes in the body of a diseased recipient; (2) by the phenomena of light connected with it: Sensitives see the odic luminosities when awake in a dark room, somnambulists in sleep without a dark room; (3) by various phenomena of motion caused by the odic radiations; for instance, the deviation of the magnetic needle, etc.; (4) by chemical changes on the photographic plate. But, as if nothing had been done, voices are still heard which deny magnetism.

"It is sometimes said that the effects of magnetism are merely the results of suggestion; that a patient is not cured by imparting the vitality of another, but by the influence of his mind, or auto-suggestion. These objections, however, are extremely narrow-minded, because they regard the suggestion which I give to the patient as a conception of the brain and nothing more. This mere conception, as such, cannot effect a cure, but acts only in cases in which the brain of the recipient has at its command a sufficient amount of vital power, which can be directed to the diseased portion of the body designated by the suggestion. In mesmeric healing the vital power of the magnetiser is communicated to another organism; in healing by suggestion the magnetism of the patient himself is put in motion, and guided to the seat of the disease. Whoever affirms that the mere conception of the brain can heal without any mediating power between the brain and the seat of disease, asserts an effect without a cause."

Since the physicists of the University of Nancy, France, Charpentier and Blondlot, have informed the Paris Academy of Sciences that they have succeeded in fixing in the human body rays of light similar to those emitted by the mysterious substance radium, the learning of the schools will soon be convinced of human healing magnetism. We are now living in a time when—remember merely the discoveries of Hittorf, Crookes, Röntgen, Becquerel, Curie and Le Bon—new phenomena of light and waves of ether are constantly being reported. But, unfortunately, the words of Schiller concerning professional scholars still apply to the majority of physicians: "Every expansion of the science by which he earns his living makes him uneasy, because it sends him new work or makes his past labour useless, every important innovation startles him, for it destroys the old school method which he mastered with so much toil; it exposes him to the danger of losing all the work of his past life. Who has cried out against reformers more than the throng of professional scholars? Who checks the progress of useful revolutions in the realm of knowledge more than these same men? Every light kindled by a successful genius, no matter in what branch of science it may be, makes their insufficiency visible; they fight with bitter anger, with malice, with despair, because, with the school system which they are defending, they are fighting for their whole existence. Therefore, there is no more implacable foe, no more envious official colleague, no more willing persecutor, than the professional scholar."*

After having now seen a large number of mediums of all kinds, I must admit, that even where the performances are genuine, a large portion of their statements always rests upon telepathy. This fact can and ought not to be shut out; they say that we should like to hear

---

*Schiller's Works, Cotta, 1877, 4th edition, p. 214, and following: "What is and for what purpose do we study Universal History?" An academic commencement speech.

what lies in our own consciousness, that is what we hope will come. There are, it is true, rare exceptions—I have known such—but even with these the factor of telepathy should be absolutely reckoned with, if we wish to move safely. The member of the Reichstag Stocker is not so entirely wrong when he warns us of the perils, that is, of the abuse of Spiritualism.* It is a two-edged sword, and only people of responsible character and scientific education ought to occupy themselves with it. Whoever does not stand on a firm footing may easily be led into by-paths by placing implicit confidence in mediums, whose statements are solely the reflection of his own ideas, so far as the matter concerns the so-called revelations of Spiritualism. Professor Crookes wrote very aptly concerning this in 1874 to a Russian lady, who had asked him whether he was a Spiritualist as follows:

"All that I am convinced of is, that invisible and intelligent beings exist, who say that they are the spirits of dead persons. But proof that they really are the individuals they assume to

---

*See *Uebersinnliche Welt* (Transcendental World), August-September, 1900, p. 355, and *Psychical Studies*, 1900, p. 186.

be, which I require in order to believe it, I have never received, though I am disposed to admit that many of my friends assert that they have actually obtained the desired proofs, and I myself have already frequently been many times on the verge of this conviction."*

Mystification is one of the most frequent phenomena of spiritualism. But is there no genuine coin because some is counterfeit? It is much to be regretted that the classified works of Rochas have not yet been translated into English. He has shown that from the living human being an inner essence of being may be separated, which lives on, feels, works and thinks, so the experimental proof of immortality is already present in Animism. A Kardec has been translated, while translations of such eminently important and undoubtedly valuable scientific investigations are still delayed, which may perhaps be explained, at least partially, by the fact that the representatives of official science at the third International Psychological Congress, held in Munich in 1896, represented a psychology without psyche. True, hundreds

---

*Professor Angelo Brofferio: *Für den Spiritismus* (In Behalf of Spiritualism), Leipzig, Max Spohr, 1894, p. 319.

of foreign scholars of the first rank who upheld metaphysics could be cited; but official science, especially in Germany, still considers it "bad form" to be interested in it. But the time is drawing nearer, when we shall be able to say "Sic derisa diu tandem bona causa triumphat" (Thus at last truth, long derided, triumphed).

Therefore, the deep thinker, Dr. du Prel, correctly remarks: "From the standpoint of materialism, to which love and marriage are only physical, but not metaphysical—which opinion Alexander von Humboldt* is also said to have held—marriage appears a crime; for parents have no right, for their own pleasure, to bring a new being into this existence, for such beings, lacking the metaphysical background could only be regarded as impostures. Only when love is identical with the transcendental act of will of the being pressing into life, is marriage to be justified."† Therefore let whoever wishes to approach the grave, wavering figures from another world, do so always with doubting, investigating mind, this will do no harm; but

---

*See Mainländer: *Philosophie der Erlösung* (Philosophy of the Redemption), I, p. 349.
†Du Prel: *Die Philosophie der Mystik* (The Philosophy of Mysticism), Leipsic, Günther, p. 472.

whoever does not feel his heart joyfully stirred by their approach, even finds it unpleasant because distrust has its root there, let him avoid them, for he cannot detain them. We human beings of flesh and blood also like to stay only where we are welcome.

On the 19th of August, 1905, I found occasion to visit the newly discovered gold fields of Nevada. The trip there is somewhat complicated, for though Nevada joins California, there is no direct road, but one must go by way of San Francisco to reach Reno in Nevada, from which three different companies have built a branch road to Tonopah. From Los Angeles to Tonopah is a journey of two days and two nights. Whoever wishes to go east or north from San Francisco must cross the bay twice. First to Oakland on a ferry boat, then the road runs for an hour along the bay to Port Costa, where the whole train is placed on a steam ferry boat which carries it across the bay to the station of Benicia on the other side. Such a transportation of an entire train upon a ship across the water is very interesting for a novice. A boat of this kind will take thirty-eight freight, or twenty passenger, cars at once. Here the bay is calm, but on my journey to Alaska our train was also carried on a ferry boat across the Columbia river between Portland and Tacoma, where it is wide and rapid. I cannot remember ever having been transported in Europe in this way.

The way from Reno to Tonopah is at first extremely pretty, but then it enters the desert; true, mountains (the eastern side of the Sierra Nevada) are visible on both sides, but otherwise the route is dreary, only Lake Walker, forty miles long, giving a little variety.

Tonopah is a gold-mining city in the true sense of the word. Saloons, tingle tangle, gambling houses with roulette à la Monte Carlo, only here one does not see thousand-franc notes, but one-dollar coins, principally in tents or wooden sheds, dirty and destitute of any touch of refinement. I slept at a so-called hotel (Merchant Hotel) in a room which the dairy maid at Nussdorf at the inn in Upper Bavaria, where, in 1897, I lodged with a mountain peasant, would have refused to occupy.*

---

*The worst hotel I encountered on my travels was at Vera Cruz, on the Gulf of Mexico, for that had not even a roof. In Central Egypt, the excrements are covered with sand, instead of being treated with water,

The whole country around Tonopah is worked by the gold-seekers, and the desert sand whirls through these extremely primitive hamlets. From Tonopah automobiles run to Goldfield through the deserts, whose soil consists of rock covered with pebbles and sand, so that the trip of thirty-one miles to Goldfield can be made in two hours. It is a peculiar feeling to pass at sunset in an automobile through the wilderness. Nothing grows there except dried bushes, and here and there the yucca palm.

Goldfield is a city of tents, in a deep valley through which the sand continually whirls. But I was obliged to go farther to the Ralston desert, between Goldfield and Bullfrog. A tent in the midst of the wilderness was my lodging for the night.

The Goldfield mines, in less than two years, have produced more than four million dollars in gold. The worst feature is the lack of water, which must be brought in casks twenty miles by waggon to the Ralston desert; but, nevertheless, everybody flocks there, and there is now a road being built to Goldfield. Rattlesnakes and liz-

---

which, it is true, is well there, because water is usually lacking.

ards are the only creatures that live there, and it is fortunate that the rattlesnakes leave their hiding-places only in the hot noonday, otherwise one might have very unpleasant visitors in an open tent at night.

In the desert of Nevada, as formerly in the Libyan wilderness in Egypt, I suffered the magnificence of nature at sunset to exert its influence upon my spirit. Camille Flammarion,* Professor of Astronomy in Paris, says in his book concerning the boundlessness of space: "Let us imagine ourselves carried with the swiftness of the ray of light, which is 77,000 leagues (in round numbers about 40,000 geographical miles) in a second away from the earth toward a point in the heavens. A second passes—77,000 leagues are left behind, another —154,000! Let us hasten on. Ten seconds, a minute, ten minutes—50 million leagues lie behind us. We go on an hour, a day, a week, without pausing in our flight, whole months, a year—the space which we have traversed is already so great that, if we wish to express it in kilometers, the number is so incomprehensible

---

*Camille Flammarion: *Les merveilles célestes* (Celestial Wonders), Paris, 1865.

that it conveys nothing to our power of perception—there are trillions, millions upon millions. Where are we?

"We have left behind long ago the last of the stars visible from the earth; we have long been in other, unknown, unexplored spheres. No number can fix the space behind; thousands of millions upon thousands of millions are nothing in comparison to this measureless expanse,— our ability of comprehension is wearied. But what is still more incomprehensible is—we have not advanced even one step in space."

At the thought of these beautiful words of Flammarion, and the infinity which surrounds us, I fully realized the pettiness of human prejudices and the utter desolation of a view of the world which will admit nothing but materialism, while the scientific representatives of metapsychics prove that their opponents foist upon them their own unpleasant opinions by passing over the most convincing proofs in silence, and disputing facts which no one maintains, in order at last, forced to recognize absolutely irrefutable phenomena, to attribute them to a force absolutely incapable of producing them.

An interesting incident of the seance of October 24, 1905, was that we suddenly heard a great number of voices behind the curtain. Betsy said that once Egyptian women, and another time Indians, had come in crowds to show this phenomenon. On October 29 and November 2 I sent for the photographer, Edward Wyllie, San Francisco, 875 Sutter Street, in order to see what the photographic plate would receive. The pictures were taken by flashlight, and were very remarkable. Besides the materialized figures, the development showed a number of spirits who could not be previously seen with the eyes. In one picture I instantly recognized an uncle of mine, whom I had converted to Spiritualism by another medium about twelve years before. He now came from gratitude, as Betsy told me. I have already sent these pictures to de Rochas, since at present France appears to me to stand at the head of the Spiritualistic movement; at least, in consequence of its progress there, men of greater scientific prominence are now studying these phenomena.

In reply to my question why more of the beings whom I knew, especially relatives and those with whom I believed I stood in intellectual relations, because I was following almost the same path as they, were not seen in these pictures, I received the reply that the beings nearly connected with me were too highly developed, so that they no longer worked in the material sphere, but rather in the sphere of inspiration, and it would be easier for them to control trance or speech mediums.

As soon as hunger, sensual love, and property* lose their importance in the intelligible world—that is, to our real being—because they possess them only for the cell-body (of the present life), the foundation and cause of our social distinctions will also disappear; the ideas of wealth and aristocracy, nay, even of age and youth, will have no meaning, for they are phantoms. Distinctions will probably exist, but of a different kind, because the principle of classification is different. That is (regarded from the standpoint of our real being), a large portion of

---

*As is well known, Proudhon said that private property was robbery, and St. Benedict, in his famous rule of the Order (Chapters 33 and 55, Salmansweiler, 1791, pages 112 and 168), calls it the most malicious crime. (Baron von Hellenbach's Social Politics, *Sphinx,* Gera, Reuss, 1890, p. 260.)

everything which men consider the greatest blessings of life, will disappear.

I also again had occasion to admire the medical knowledge of Star Eagle. At the first seance he told me that my "magnetism" was red instead of blue, and I was suffering from urocystitis. True, he did not use this medical professional term, but his description of my sharp pains was perfect. Here help must be obtained at once, and he would bring me the next day a liquid, which I must take immediately. The following day he really did come, and I distinctly heard,—since for this experiment almost total darkness must reign,—drops fall into a phial; then he laid the bottle on my head and gave it to me. On the second day after, the violet, stinging pains had disappeared! He told me that this liquid was an extract from about three hundred herbs, principally East Indian ones, and that a large number of spirits had had to help him to prepare the remedy and give it to me in a material form.

Occult literature often describes such cases, but the majority of physicians will not hear of anything of the kind. There must be no competition, though the doctors often err in diagnoses, as well as in therapeutics. Somnambulism, mediumism, swindling! But these gentlemen have not even dreamed of all these things as they really are! In America, there is far more toleration; almost the larger number of educated people know something of it; there need be no constraint in mentioning the subject in the best society, and even in the daily papers and magazines one often reads descriptions from the province of metaphysics, so that supporters and opponents have an opportunity to speak.

In the seance previously mentioned, where Jemima Clark, as a muslin ball, rolled up my left leg to my heart, and finally materialized outside of the cabinet before our eyes, a Frenchman, M. Priet, whose wife, an ardent follower of Mr. Miller, was also present, came as a materialized phantom, and I heard his voice. He had died about ten weeks before, while traveling in France. I knew him in life, and he now, as a spirit, regretted that he had not, while on earth, become better acquainted with Spiritualism, like his wife. I have quite frequently heard such regret for similar neglect expressed by spiritual beings. Their companions in life had usually suffered enough from the derision of such people, and regret in such cases comes too late!

The historically authentic material upon spiritualistic phenomena is on the whole so great, that already a thoroughly superficial judge of it does not know whether to wonder most over the ignorance or the thoughtlessness of such antagonists.

Mr. Stead, the editor in chief of the *"Pall Mall Gazette,"* and the *"Review of Reviews,"* well known as the champion of the friends of peace and by his free disclosures of the sins of the so-called fashionable world, points out that, during the last quarter of a century, more than three thousand spiritualistic works have appeared—among them forty-six scientific periodicals in all languages—and that the number of Spiritualists of European races has already exceeded fifty millions! And, in addition, there are the fifty thousand Theosophists who follow Mme. Blavatsky!*

That these things do not undergo an objective

---

*Von Werth: *Moderne Magie* (Modern Magic) in "Sphinx," 1895, p. 156, Brunswick, C. A. Schwetschke & Son.

critical examination from the majority of those who wish to represent exact science, is evidently due to the fact that our "men of science" are still for the most part involved in prejudices, for there are not only stupid and superstitious prejudices, but, as is well known, also scientific prejudices. In the presence of this vast amount of historical material, the crushing testimony of the living generation, and the absurdity of the materialistic assumption of a "thinking albumen," the opponents of Spiritualism to-day might rather be called men of scientific delusions.

In Mr. Miller's seances, the control, Betsy, always came at the close of the sitting and said a few farewell words. During the whole seance, she said she was obliged to help the spirits who wished to materialize, since, especially for newcomers, this was difficult to accomplish, and still more difficult to appear in the same features they had had on earth, which is conceivable, and every one can try on himself. For if one has not seen himself in the glass for some time, it might be difficult for most people to remember accurately the lines of their faces; then how is it to be done as a spirit, when the personality has disappeared?

Very interesting things have often happened to me in connection with this matter. A gentleman whom I knew in life, and whom I could recognize very well as a spirit, came without the pointed beard which he formerly wore. At my inquiry, he replied that, on account of my question, he now remembered it, but, being engaged in developing his body, he had been obliged to tax his memory very severely, in order to recall every detail of his former earthly form.

Betsy, whose hand I once tried to clasp in farewell, told me laughing that she had no arms that day; she had only materialized her head and breast; there was no power left for more, because too many spirits had materialized in this seance. If we read the views of the antagonists, we marvel that such people should give any opinion at all. Scarcely one of them has ever seen a genuine medium, or conducted any experiments, and therefore such persons are not qualified to argue. Such attacks are now only laughable, and the more laughable the higher the Olympian summits from which they emanate!

We still hear most frequently the words, "Transcendental intercourse is contrary to the laws of nature." Yet, as Professor Virchow says, "What we call the law of nature is mutable, because its discovery is *human work* and its recognition results only from the best knowledge. But *later experiences* are fully qualified to overthrow entirely existing laws, and produce those great changes in the natural sciences in which modern times are so extremely rich."

VII.

On April 18th the frightful catastrophe at San Francisco occurred. I also felt a short shock at Los Angeles on the 19th, just as I was cutting a palm-tree in the garden; in the early morning, at five o'clock, black clouds with ashes had been seen to draw over Los Angeles, a thing which seldom occurs in the almost constantly cloudless sky. There are also earth-heavings at times in Southern California (the so-called cold earthquakes, produced by the drying and contraction of the interior of the earth, and not of volcanic origin), but people there are accustomed to them, and the houses are almost all built of wood, so that they yield to the shocks and are seldom damaged. The newspapers in the Eastern States published many stupid errors, which I afterwards found copied into the German papers, such as that Santa Catalina Island, in the Pacific Ocean, had disappeared, and that the port of Los Angeles had been overwhelmed by a tidal wave, like Galveston on the Gulf of Mexico. Los Angeles is about eighteen miles from the sea.

On May 16th I took my passage on a steamer of the Pacific Coast Steamship Co., in order to go from Los Angeles to San Francisco. A railway accident in the previous November, at Santa Margarita station, between Santa Barbara and San Francisco, in which two persons were killed and eleven wounded—I myself got off with a fright—had given me a distaste for the journey by rail. On May 17th, at four in the afternoon, we reached the Bay of San Francisco. The Cliff House, which is seen soon after passing the Golden Gate, is still standing, and the seals still sun themselves on the cliffs in front, while the azure heavens are mirrored just as ever in the lightly curling waves of this noble bay. Oakland, Berkeley, Alameda, etc., are seen as before, lying like pearls in the sunshine on the slopes of the ridges, and at last our steamer rounds the last promontory and San Francisco is in sight—or at least the place where it once stood!

It is a frightful sight from a distance—a heap of ruins, which is still partly smoking, four weeks after the catastrophe. Even the pier, to which our steamer makes fast, is half burnt away, and the "Spokane," in which I went to Alaska in 1905, lies at the pier, converted into a hotel, for not one is left in San Francisco.

Bulwer relates how Glaucus, Ione, and Nydia wandered about in the ruins of Pompeii; many thus wander about in San Francisco, seeking friends and acquaintances, mainly in vain, for nearly three-quarters of the city is a heap of ashes, and about 250,000 people have had to leave it already. How many have met their deaths will probably never be known. From 500 to 2000 persons are believed to have been burnt to death, or buried under the ruins. Eye-witnesses of this terrible event told me that no pen could describe the horrors of the scene, when the inhabitants were aroused from sleep at 5:15 on the morning of the 18th of April by the first shock, and their houses began to tumble about their ears. Twenty thousand buildings were destroyed, including the great stores and office buildings in the business quarter of the city. The next result was that conflagrations broke out everywhere, against which the fire brigade was powerless, because the water-pipes had been broken by the powerful earthquake shock.

Among the fine buildings thus destroyed I may mention the City Hall, which had cost about seven million dollars, the Palace Hotel, the *Call* Building, the *Chronicle* Building, the *Examiner* Building, the Post Office, the Hobart Building, the Grand Opera House, the Lick House, the Nevada Bank Block, the St. Francis Hotel, the Mark Hopkins Museum with all its art treasures, etc. The interesting Chinatown has disappeared. One might walk for hours among heaps of ruins, and see many safes, which offered no resistance to the fire, but were burnt out. The flames reached a height of 200 feet, and made night like day.

The help afforded by the United States filled me with admiration and respect. Railway trains poured in uninterruptedly from all quarters to Oakland with provisions, for there were about 400,000 people to be taken care of gratuitously, and this was done! I myself stood in the so-called bread-line, where thousands took their places every day to receive meat, potatoes, milk and crackers free of cost, for nobody had any money, the banks dared not open their vaults for four weeks, in order to allow them to cool, and there were no longer any stores in existence where people could buy anything.

San Francisco will be rebuilt, and this may take five or ten years. Care will be taken to provide a better water-supply, and the world so easily forgets. I heard people say that this frightful catastrophe was a punishment sent by God for San Francisco's immorality. Certainly there was a considerable amount of loose life in San Francisco, as in all seaport towns. Almost the whole trade between Japan, China, the Sunda Islands, Australia, etc., and the United States passes through San Francisco; a portion also through Seattle and Vancouver, and where so many nationalities come together, morals are not often very strict.

Davis says, "God cannot go outside of the laws He has imposed," but the finite can never come to understand the Infinite! In my account of my travels I have spoken of the unfreedom of humanity, and in connection with what I have said as to the need for critical consideration of the comparative value of spirit communications, I wish to mention the explanation of a similar catastrophe which was given by an excarnate being. I had several conversations with this spirit, and his explanations were far from being commonplace. I think it was in 1894, when an ocean steamship went down with all on board; I asked this spirit why God had not saved even one of them. The answer was, that it was the destiny of the ship and all the people on board to meet their end on that day, and by water. All these passengers had been so guided that they came together on that ship, whose foundering was destined from the day on which it was launched, and in this way they were summoned, as du Prel says, to suffer the fate they had themselves chosen. But I do not care to concern myself with this hypothesis.

As regards Mr. Miller, his place of business and dwelling-house are both burnt to the ground. What once was Bush Street is now a waste and a heap of ruins. An employé of his, Charley Kleebauer, whom I found, told me that Miller had received a letter from his father saying that his mother was very sick, and that he must come to Nancy (France) at once if he wished to see her again. Miller thinks a great deal of his mother, and started for Nancy on the 12th of April. I wrote to him to seek out Colonel de Rochas, but I am unable to judge whether, after receiving the news of his loss in San Francisco, and the probable effect on his nerves, he is in a condition to give sittings.

It was my original intention to visit the Sandwich Islands and Japan in May, 1906, but was forced by unforeseen obstacles to postpone this plan. I therefore was able to pay a visit to the Eastern States, which I did not yet know, for on my arrival at New York, in 1902, I had left for the West three days afterwards.

As I wished to remain in Southern California until the first of August, on July 20th I visited Mount Wilson in the Sierra Madre Mountains, where the well-known Carnegie Observatory is situated. From the place called Sierra Madre a mule has to be taken, and the summit of Mount Wilson, which is 6000 feet high, is reached in about five hours. The trail is rather dangerous, for it is mostly only wide ʻenough for a mule, and in places leads along the edge of precipices a thousand feet deep. It was night when I got to the top, and I could not see my hand before my eyes, but the mule knew the way, and I simply let him go.

Very wonderful is the view at night from the top of Mount Wilson over Los Angeles, which lies at a distance of about fifteen miles. From this height one sees in the distance, like a Fata Morgana, a sea of electric flames, enclosed by a sky as black as night. In January, 1902, as I rode back along the Nile towards Assouan from the Temple of Isis, on the Island of Philæ, shaded with sycamores and palms, along the barrage at Assouan, which is one of those wonders which have an overpowering effect, I had a similar view in full sunlight. Like a phantasmagoria I saw in the distance, in the midst of the sands of the Libyan Desert, the ruins of a place which, under the reflection of the sunlight and the glowing waste of sand, looked like a ghostly city. Yet Assouan is now full of Europeans and Americans, and on the spot where Herodotus and Strabo once stood in wonder before the ancient nilometer, which is still in existence, may now be seen the "globe-trotters" of the whole world.

On the first of August, just the date on which I came to Southern California four years before, I journeyed northward, and it is a remarkable fact that every fourth year I experienced important changes. So on this occasion, I quitted California in order to reside further east. I can count back for the last twenty years how every four years important events have entered into my life, so that Baron Hellenbach's *Magic of Numbers* (Vienna, 1882) seems to be no empty fancy.

On December 14th I came back to Southern California, in order to arrange various affairs before my final removal to the East, and can indeed say that my long stay in the Eastern States had brought me much that was new. I had special opportunities for meeting Theosophists of all shades of thought, and found that they had many beautiful ideas. Ethics, philosophy, and practice for self-development, are the essential points. The basis of the whole doctrine is rebirth, and I must agree with Prof. Seiling when he says, "The solving of the riddle of humanity will be brought much nearer through the doctrine of reincarnation, together with that of Karma." I must also admit that du Prel's dictum, that the life is self-ordained by the transcendental self, does not altogether hold good; for there are lives whose course can scarcely be regarded as voluntarily self-ordained, but are rather to be understood as the outworking of an unalterable law.

But here a question comes forward, as to which I can obtain no enlightenment. According to my experience, Astrology rests on a true basis, but the moment of birth is not subject to the mother's control. How does this influence of the stars on human fate agree with the law of Karma? According to the law of Karma we must expiate the debt of guilt which we have contracted in a previous life, or in the present one, and yet we are dependent on the influence of the stars, which cross our path favourably or unfavourably. The answer given to me by a Theosophist, that we can so develop ourselves that we can become masters of the stellar influences, appears to me very problematical. Moreover, in this matter, I seemed to be confronted by a hideous Janus-head. One of those gentlemen, who seems to be tolerably well read, and has established classes, in which he asserts that through vibrations clairvoyance and clairaudience can be developed, told me in all seriousness that when the new "world-cycle" began, his powers would be so much developed that he could dematerialize the hidden wealth of the Catholic Church, and re-materialize it again in order to use it for Theosophical purposes and for the building of a Theosophical temple on the Sierra Nevada in Southern California! Among a lot of other preposterous stuff he told me (in fact, he relates to all who consult him the most wonderful stories of his former incarnations) that I had been a ruler in Atlantis, and had, in foreknowledge of the destruction of that continent and of the knowledge of that period, which far surpassed our present science, hidden papers, containing memoranda about the lost Atlantis, in a cave in the mountains of Washington State, near the Pacific Ocean, that they had withstood the disintegrating effects of thousands of years, and that I should shortly rediscover them and easily decipher them, by "perception!" Also in a former incarnation I was said to be the father of Christ, and so forth. Such are the distorted forms of spiritual teaching even among American Theosophists.

Indeed the fabled Atlantis plays a great part in Theosophical circles; there is a whole literature in connection with it, said to have been given through writing mediumship. Yet there are many fine and elevated ideas on this subject. I myself, in a sitting with Miller in 1905, saw a brilliantly shining materialised spirit, eight feet high, who claimed that he was a former inhabitant of Atlantis.

After this digression I will now relate as briefly as possible the following experiences. The distance from the Pacific to the Atlantic Ocean is about 3300 miles, and it takes five days and five nights to reach New York from Southern California. A long journey, and not without danger, for the American railroads are not so safe as the European ones; even the New York *Staats-Zeitung* of Sept. 26th, 1906, gave, under the headline, "Frightful Record," a list of railroad accidents, according to which 26 persons were killed and 238 injured on an average every day on the American railroads.

On August 2nd, 1906, I reached San Francisco by boat, for the second time since the earthquake; it was not much changed in appearance during the time. According to the Report of the Special Committee of the Board of Trustees of the Chamber of Commerce, the loss at San Francisco amounted to about 350 million dollars, of which about 80 per cent. would be paid by the insurance companies.

On the 4th of August, I started on my eastward journey, and in Utah encountered the first rain. In California it does not rain from April to November, and therefore it is rather pleasant to meet with a shower of rain in summer. In Southern California, outside of the gardens, which have to be watered every day, and then exhibit quite a tropical beauty, all the vegetation assumes a grey tint in summer. After passing Salt Lake, which is 45 miles wide, and on which the Mormons have their headquarters, I reached Chicago in three days.

As I desired to go on to Buffalo by steamer, I had to stay three days in Chicago before the boat started. Though Chicago is rather a smoky and dirty city, one feels nearer to civilization there. The Art Institute of Chicago, and other temples of art, brought me back to the conditions of existence to which I had formerly been accustomed, and the raging din in the Board of Trade reminded me of the Berlin Stock Exchange, before settlement speculations were forbidden by law. Lincoln Park, with its zoological garden, is very beautiful.

On August 11th I went on board the "Northland," of the Northern Steamship Company, for the voyage along the Great Lakes, Michigan, Huron, and Erie, which takes two and a half days. The boat stops at Milwaukee, Harbor Springs, Mackinac Island (a summer resort for the people of the adjoining states), Detroit, and Cleveland, where Dr. Cyriax, editor of the *Neue Spiritualistische Blatter,* formerly published at Berlin, lived for a long time. The shores of these lakes are generally flat, and though they cannot be compared with those of the great European lakes and the Mediterranean, yet they are restful after the long journey from the Pacific.

On arriving at Buffalo, I took a car ride of about half an hour to Niagara Falls, one of the great wonders of the world. These Falls have now become a fashionable summer resort for thousands of people; even excursionists with their wives and families camp there with their perambulators. The electric car runs by the so-called Great Gorge Route, along the Whirlpool Rapids, where Captain Webb lost his life in his attempt to swim them on July 24th, 1883. At the Horseshoe Fall, on the Canadian side, I went down in an elevator, dressed as a miner, and had the Falls right over me. It is a splendid sight, to see these immense masses of water pouring down from three sides.

VIII.

Returning to Buffalo, I travelled to Dunkirk, in order to visit the Spiritualist Camp at Lily Dale. I stayed three days there in 1902, without seeing much that was very remarkable. This time I stopped there from August 15th to September 6th, and have much to relate that is of interest. Lily Dale is in Chautauqua County, on Cassadaga Lake, surrounded by ancient woods. It has an auditorium for 1500 persons and a library of 1300 books, mostly presented by mediums, and about 182 cottages. In the forenoon the Psychic Classes are held, in which lectures are given on the "psychic spheres;" there are also Physical Culture classes for the body, music several times daily, sometimes also dances in the Auditorium, so that there is something to satisfy everybody.

My first visit was to Pierre Keeler, the celebrated "Independent Slate-writing Medium." His prospectus bears many names of well-known people who have endorsed his mediumship, such as Professor Elliot Coues, Dr. Alfred Russel Wallace, Prof. Wm. Denton, and others. Mr. Keeler takes two slates, and after the sitter has wiped them himself with a wet sponge, he places one upon the other and asks the sitter to write questions for the spirits on small pieces of paper, fold them up so that Keeler can see nothing of what has been written, and then lay them on the edge of the slates. Then Keeler himself takes the pencil in his hand and writes —in my case correctly—the names of the spirits to whom the questions have been addressed (I had written five, of which he could not himself have thought). He explained to me that he is clairaudient; his control tells him these names, and these spirits are now present, though invisible. Then he tied the two slates together, and gave them into my hand, so that he held them by two corners and I by the two others, in full noon sunlight, about a foot above the table. Then I heard marvellously rapid writing, and raps, whereupon Mr. Keeler handed me the slates with the remark that the sitting (which cost two dollars) was at an end.

I went out with the slates, untied the knots in

the park, and found five separate messages, written backwards and forwards, with the signatures of those to whom I had addressed the questions. This phenomenon is very interesting in itself, for fraud on Mr. Keeler's part appears to be out of the question; some of the replies were in German, whereas Mr. Keeler, as far as I can gather from himself and others whom I have asked, is quite ignorant of that language; moreover he enjoys a very good reputation in the opinion of those likely to know. The five answers to my questions were in quite different handwritings; but they were certainly not from the persons whom I had addressed, and by whom they were signed! It is an old experience, that spirits give themselves false names, and I scarcely believe that every excarnate spirit has the capacity to write between slates; that requires a certain degree of skill, which must be acquired by practice.*

---

*Compare Dr. Robert Friese, *Stimmen aus dem Reiche der Geister* (Leipzig, 1897, Oswald Mutze) and *Das Leben jenseits des Grabes* (ib. 1893).

Mr. Hereward Carrington, member of the Council of the American Society for Scientific Research, in his book entitled *The Physical Phenomena of Spiritualism* (Small, Maynard & Co., Boston), designated Mr. Keeler as a trickster and explained in detail every manœuvre indulged in by Keeler in his alleged nefari-

An Occultist's Travels.

I next visited Mrs. J. de Bartholomew, Trumpet and Trance Medium. The room was entirely darkened, so that the trumpet through which the spirits were said to speak could never be seen. The first to speak was said to be an Indian, who gave his name as Black Hawk, and reminded me that he had spoken to me at Miller's, which I afterwards remembered was the case. As there is an interesting story connected with this Indian, I will relate it, just as "Betsy," Mr. Miller's chief control, told it to me. In 1905, I changed my residence in Southern California, and soon afterwards had occasion to see Mr. Miller in San Francisco. Among others Black Hawk came at that interview. Though I was not interested in his coming, I asked Betsy afterwards what this Indian wanted. Her answer was, that he was the chief of a band of Indians who had lived on the site of my former dwelling; they had followed me into the new house, because the purchaser of the former one was not to their liking. (Nor did living people like him much!) This In-

---

ous performances. Should Mr. Keeler have a desire to still inspire confidence and have people believe that he is an honest medium he would naturally have to subject himself to the most severe test conditions.

dian and his band took a great interest in all my affairs and pursuits. He now came again through Mrs. Bartholomew, and was very glad to be able to speak to me; he first asked me if I liked him, and I readily assented. Then I asked him how my dog Moppel was, at home. He replied that he was all right, but that I had now two dogs. This was correct, for five months before I had bought a St. Bernard dog. To my second question, what readers in Germany of my travel experiences thought of me, I received an answer which made me laugh heartily, namely, that some thought I was crazy, because some things that I had written about Miller's sittings were impossible. It is evident that Black Hawk has at any rate an open and candid character! After him an Atlantean spirit manifested, who spoke earnestly of reincarnation as a truth. It was at any rate curious that an entity should hold forth on reincarnation, just at the time when I had been giving a great deal of consideration to the question of its possibility.

The third medium I visited was Mrs. L. Evelyn Barr, also a "trumpet medium," but she holds her sittings in full daylight. This sitting was in some respects the most interesting of all to me, for well-known names were spoken through the trumpet. Yet Mr. Keeler, the slate-writing medium above mentioned, knew these names, and I was told that mediums had what is called a "blue-book," in which are noted down the names of all visitors, and of the spirits after whom they have inquired. I will not accuse Mrs. Barr of having been in personal communication with Mr. Keeler for this purpose, because I cannot prove anything; but I cannot deny that I was suspicious, because the spirits who announced themselves were the very ones with whom I had wished to speak through Mr. Keeler.

The directors of Lily Dale are very strict with regard to mediums suspected of fraudulent practices. While I was there, Dr. K., who gave "demonstrations of unseen forces" in the Auditorium, and did astonishing things, suddenly disappeared. The directors had asked him to leave the camp, because there was reason to suspect that he had made use of such a "blue-book."

Miss F. M. C. Cottrill, a young lady, who is a medium for raps, makes an excellent impression, but gives no public performances for earning money. Wherever she stands, there are raps in full sunlight, even on cement, pillows, etc. She would be a good subject for the scientific researchers!

I also visited Mrs. W. Ripley, trance speaker and clairvoyant, who obtained excellent results in a circle of ten persons. Another medium, Mr. Charles S. Hulbert, held his trance discourses in the midst of the woods. On the second occasion he had the misfortune, after a very acceptable speech on the theory of descent, to be controlled by a negro girl, who gradually dropped into an indelicate way of speaking, so that the ladies who were present left, and were soon followed by the men. The poor man told me the next day that he remained entranced so long that it was midnight before he got home from the woods, and that when he awoke he could not understand why he was all alone, because at the beginning of the sitting he was surrounded with people. This experience is a good proof of the genuineness of Mr. Hulbert's mediumship, for in his waking state he is incapable of talk of this description.

I afterwards became acquainted with Mrs.

J. Werner; she calls herself a healer, from Allegheny, Pa.; she is clairvoyant and makes diagnoses. She is assistant to Dr. G. Leonard Le-Van, who also was with her at Lily Dale. She is rather an agreeable person, and she told me I ought not to eat tomatoes, because my kidneys were weak. In fact, I had kidney pains at the time.

An honourable place in my account of Lily Dale must be accorded to Mrs. Elise Stumpf, Inspirational Speaker and Magnetic Healer. A German by birth, she has in former years written much for the paper *Lichtstrahlen* of Chicago. She devoted herself to the interests of the Camp, and has the best qualities of character. Anyone needing encouragement and comfort will get what they need from her. There are also a number of other mediums, but of less importance.

I must now say something about Mrs. Cora L. V. Richmond, Pastor of the Church of the Soul at Chicago. As an inspirational speaker she has the best-known name in the United States. A thick volume of 759 pages* has been

---

*Lifework of Mrs. Cora L. V. Richmond, by Harrison D. Barrett, published under the auspices of the

published about her by the National Spiritualists' Association of the U. S. A. Since she was eleven years old, so it is stated, she has given lectures upon Spiritualism under inspiration, and even in different languages. I heard her speak in the Auditorium on "Astro-psychology," that is, the influence of the intelligences of the stars upon men, when the latter are born at a time which renders them sensitive to such influences. She denies the influences of the stars themselves, and teaches that of the inhabitants of the planets, such as Mars, Saturn, Jupiter, Venus, and the Asteroids. She is now 66 years old, and during all these years she has spoken under inspiration on all branches of knowledge. She speaks excellently, and is very attractive in appearance. Her husband takes down her discourses by stenography, so that they may not be lost.

Mrs. Richmond speaks very quietly and impressively, but expresses herself too decidedly about unverifiable themes. She must pardon me, but with all respect for her work, which must often have aroused strong contestation,

---

National Spiritualists' Association of the U. S. A. Chicago: Hack & Anderson, 1895.

one should not make assertions which are impossible of proof in such a categorical tone. Her husband told me that she delivered her discourses in trance. Now from my childhood and through my formerly very extensive practice all phases of trance condition and somnambulism are thoroughly known to me. Closed eyes, disappearance of the pupil of the eye, loss of sensibility, etc., are the signs of such a condition. But none of these occur with Mrs. Richmond. She speaks with her eyes open and with absolute control over her body. In my opinion she may speak under inspiration—that is quite possible—but she does not speak in trance. In mediums for inspiration, according to all experience, their own ideas easily become mingled with what is apparently "given them" from the Beyond.

I have only heard three of her discourses, and I must say, without wishing to accuse Mrs. Richmond of plagiarism, that I have read the greater part of the ideas enunciated by her in Andrew Jackson Davis's works, seventeen years ago. She also spoke of a prenatal influence on the child; I have nothing to say against this, but du Prel has written on this theme much more clearly and satisfactorily without any trance and from a scientific point of view.* She also spoke about "sun-machines;" in time people would learn how to catch the sun's rays and use them at night instead of the electric light. At the end, however, she mentioned that she was only uttering "opinions."

At Lily Dale they also held "Forest Temple Meetings." On some rising ground in the woods there are benches and a platform, from which mediums give addresses or deliver "spirit messages." I happened to meet there one day perhaps ten mediums whom I knew, and who were standing round a man who was distributing pop-corn, a favourite American delicacy. Suddenly a number of these mediums seemed to be possessed; they ran about and executed a veritable Indian dance. These mediums were really in trance and appeared to be controlled by Indians, who had formerly been killed on this spot. Dr. du Prel and Professor Perty describe similar phenomena.†

---

*Du Prel: *Die Magische Psychologie*, Jena, 1899, p. 233, and *Das Versehen*, in *Die Zukunft* (Berlin, Harden) of Nov. 16 and 23, 1895.

†Du Prel: *Die Magie als Naturwissenschaft*, Jena, 1899, p. 147. Prof. Perty, *Der jetzige Spiritismus und*

Lily Dale is all the more interesting, as it is a very prettily situated place; everything is well organized, and the management maintains, as has been remarked, a strict discipline. Mediums who are not in good repute are not admitted into this camp. I met three judges there, who gave their legal advice gratis when there was a discussion in the Auditorium about the financial arrangements. The camp is closed at the beginning of September, and some of the mediums go to spend the winter months at Lake Helen Camp, in Florida. People can, however, stay in Lily Dale in the winter, as Mr. W. H. Bach used to do when he edited the *Sunflower*, which was published there, but there was no electric light then, and people had to find their way about at night with a lantern.

On September 6th, I went by Buffalo to Albany, on the Hudson River, and thence to New York by steamer. The trip on the river, taking about eight hours, took me past the Catskill Mountains and Poughkeepsie, which are familiar to readers of A. J. Davis's *Magic Staff*. The Hudson is called the American Rhine. If

---

verwandte Erscheinungen, Leipzig and Heidelberg, 1877, p. 252.

it has no old ruined castles to show, there is very fine scenery on it, especially as New York is approached. I afterwards had great pleasure in taking a walk along the Hudson.

It is not my purpose in the present narrative of travel to give a description of New York, yet I must acknowledge that no city in the world can compare with it for beauty and grandeur. I know Berlin, Paris, London, St. Petersburg, Rome, and other great cities fairly well, but there is no city that has anything to compare with the riches of Fifth Avenue, in which so many millionaires have their palaces. Even in Paris and London I have not seen such jewelry and art stores as, for instance, Tiffany's or the Gorham Company's in Fifth Avenue. A house is being built in New York which has 42 stories. The traffic in Broad Street, where the Stock Exchange is, and in Wall Street, is quite terrific; there is the incessant mad rush of the elevated railroad overhead and of the subway beneath the feet of the people in the streets.

I must not forget to mention the quite unique libraries in this city. The University Library arouses the astonishment of the visitor from Europe by its architectural beauty, the richness of its contents, and the convenience of its arrangements; yet it is put in the shade by the public libraries. In the European cities castles and cathedrals are usually the most conspicuous architectural features; in the United States, the stranger who wishes to admire the chief architectural monuments of a place, may with confidence expect to be shown the Free Library. It is as though people wished to make up for the absence of the palaces of princes by erecting the most magnificent palaces possible for the princes of art and literature. And these sovereigns of art are not intrenched behind official bulwarks; they keep open doors and grant audiences to everyone. A noble palace of white marble is being built on Fifth Avenue for a Free Library, which is to contain the libraries founded by Lenox and Astor. Even in the wild West, in California, there are public libraries everywhere, which have been founded by some rich man.

Now as to my experiences in metapsychical matters. I remained in New York from September 8th to December 8th, and had many interesting experiences in this respect, some hardly worth mentioning, others very much more so. Herr Hermann Handrich, Secretary of the Swiss Consulate, whom I often had the pleasure of meeting, was most ready to give me information as to what New York and Brooklyn had to offer in this regard. He took me first to Eva, niece of Mr. Roach, building contractor, of 52 East Street. Her control, "Jack," gave several tests with articles placed under the table, a tambourine, mandolin, bell, and flat-iron, and with these he repeated, under the table, whatever anyone did above the table. Fraud appeared to be out of the question, because the medium sits under good conditions and not for payment. I have been present at so many of these test-sittings that I have no longer any great interest in phenomena of this sort, although I must admit that they are perhaps the only ones which, under strict observation by competent investigators, can be of service to science as verifiable occult phenomena.

On October 16, I visited for the first time the celebrated clairvoyant, Mrs. May Pepper, of Brooklyn, who is pastor of the First Spiritualist Church there. I found 38 ladies and four men, so closely packed together in a basement room that an apple could not have fallen to the ground between them. Her Tuesday and Friday sittings are so frequented that her sister, who sits at the entrance as cashier (50 cents each person) simply closes the door when there are no more chairs vacant, and many people are thus turned away. Each visitor lays a closed envelope, containing the questions to which answers are desired, on a small table, which is so heaped with them that many of them fall to the ground as soon as Mrs. Pepper, at the beginning of the seance, begins to feel among them to find the one she wants.

She usually tears off a little piece, the size of a thumb-nail, puts this into her mouth and then tells fluently what is in the letter, gives the names of living and deceased persons, which are not written in the letter, but who are connected with the contents of the letter or with the writer. She tears the veil from the past and present with such striking certainty that in the cases of some twenty persons whose letters she handled in my presence, she only made one single mistake or misconception. As a psychometric clairvoyant she is quite astounding, that is an unquestionable fact.

At my first visit my letter was not among

those dealt with, but at my second visit she came to my questions. She told me things about which I had not asked, and which no one knew, and therefore her own explanation seems to be acceptable, that she is clairvoyant and clairaudient. When she took a letter in her hand, she would say, for instance, that a spirit, whose name was So-and-So, told her this and that. I received in this way advice from a spirit to whom I had not addressed any question—and moreover he was a near relative of mine—and she said expressly that this spirit wanted her to tell me this. The principle of the method employed by materialistic philosophers, of seeking the causes of occult phenomena in the animated organism of a living person until all possibility of a "natural" explanation is excluded, is of course quite correct in itself; but Mrs. Pepper told me, as I have said, things which I had not asked at all, and did not tell me other things, which I had asked. According to my experience this is to be explained in this way, that the spirits to whom I had addressed questions were not able to get into connection with Mrs. Pepper; but on the other hand a spirit was able to do this to whom I had not put any question.

There were two ladies who would not admit that their letters contained what Mrs. Pepper asserted that they did; Mrs. Pepper had these letters opened and read by other persons, and it was plain that everything that she had asserted was correct. Mrs. Pepper revenged herself by revealing, before all present, events in the past life of one of the incredulous, or rather, dishonorable ladies, and they were things that were not suited to publicity; but Mrs. Pepper is extremely sensitive, and does not easily pardon distrust. As I have said, Mrs. Pepper is a most astonishing psychometrist. If she is right in saying that the spirits surrounding her questioners tell her everything that she utters, it would appear that these unseen spirits who are present know the past and present very well, while the future—with certain exceptions—is closed to them, or that, as I often heard it said, they dare not reveal it.

Baron Hellenbach says very justly on this point: "The supersensible world must not always give full proof of its existence, if the purpose of our being is to be fulfilled. So long as the world we know has existed in history, the presumed other world has always attracted individuals and groups of persons to it; it has never failed of indications that our actions are not to be judged from the crude animal standpoint; nevertheless, it has always abstained from saving us the trouble of meditation, and from putting an end to our doubts. It has never desired to show us all the illusory nature of our existence. For the whole of human existence would be but a superfluous, agonizing game, if men did not set themselves to solve the problems of earth life. With the consciousness of our cosmical existence we should no longer be men, because all trials would seem illusory and would lose all their value. The supersensible world can, may, and will unbosom itself—as far as it has the power—according to all reasonable grounds for belief, only to him, who through his own fulness of power has raised himself above the deception of appearances, and who, either through the penetration of his judgment or by the lofty impulse of his soul, feels the need of the Transcendental."

I also saw other mediums, but I refrain from describing their capabilities, for they were not sufficiently free from suspicion.

IX.

As chance would have it, I was still in New York when Mr. Miller returned from Europe. He made a great sensation in France and Germany. After having recovered from the shock to his nerves caused by the news of the destruction by earthquake of his property and business in San Francisco, he went to Paris, where he gave the series of seances which caused great public excitement in France, and attracted the attention of persons in Europe interested in metapsychics. Scientific journals, magazines, and daily newspapers discussed his seances in their columns: *L'Echo du Merveilleux, La Tribune Psychique, la Revue du Spiritualisme Moderne, L'Initiation,* in Paris, and *Light* in London, were especially eulogistic in their expressions. Dr. Encausse ("Papus") in *L'Initiation* for October, 1906, wrote: "All other mediums that I have seen are as little children compared to Miller." Delanne, Gaston Mery, and other well-known men and leaders in the occult movement in France, have expressed themselves in like manner.

Miller also went to Munich, Germany, and convinced the scientists in that country of his wonderful powers. Articles in *Die Uebersinnliche Welt,* Berlin, by Dr. Walter Bormann, and in *Psychische Studien,* Leipzig, October, 1906, by Colonel Peters, sounded the enthusiastic praises of Miller.

I have, however, to regret that Mr. Miller failed to become personally acquainted with Colonel de Rochas. Had the two met in seances in the sense in which de Rochas wrote to me, then the scientific world would have heard of it. As it is, the world of Spiritualism has been informed that my observations relating to Mr. Miller, as published in Germany, France, and America, were correct; but the world of science, which does not concern itself with Spiritualism, did not hear of these evidences.

In conjunction with Colonel de Rochas, I would have done everything to inform the representatives of psychology and physiology at the great universities of Europe concerning these remarkable phenomena, expecting the co-operation in our report of the several European experts who were to have been present with Colonel de Rochas. It will be an everlasting regret to me that this meeting of experts failed to take place.

I know by experience that mediums are very liable to be affected by passing moods, and that it is therefore very difficult to depend upon them. Anything that occurs to them serves to change their ideas, and one must be exceedingly careful to keep them in a good humour.

On November 2, 1906, Mr. Miller and Mr. Kleebauer, who had followed him to Europe, arrived in New York on board the "La Touraine," and I had four seances with him, the first being held on that same evening in Eighty-fourth Street. He told me that the Catholic Church had tried to make difficulties for him in France, which from my own experience I consider quite possible. The use of animal magnetism is still forbidden by an encyclical of the Holy Roman Inquisition of July 30, 1856, addressed to all the Bishops, which says: *"Quapropter Episcopi omnem impendant opem ad hujusmodi magnetismi abusus reprimendos et evellendos, ut dominicus grex defendatur et fideles sibi crediti a morum corruptione praeserventur."* (Therefore all Bishops shall use every means to suppress and prevent the use of such magnetism, that the Lord's flock may be defended and the faithful believers may be preserved from corruption of morals.) See also my book, *Der Heilmagnetismus,* 3rd edition, Berlin, 1896, p. 93.

As is sufficiently shown in the much-talked-of book by Dr. Lapponi, the recently deceased personal physician to the Pope, the Roman Catholic Church condemns Spiritualism without reservation, and for good reasons: the Church does not wish to lose her power. As the freethinker, Ernst von Wolzogen, truly says in Herr Harden's *Zukunft,* No. 52, of Sept. 29, 1906 (Berlin): "The miraculous pictures, the processions, the Immaculate Queen of Heaven, the doctrine of purgatory and the great number of easily accessible saints as intermediaries of earthly wishes before the heavenly throne, all these are strong pillars of the Church's power." In 1897, I treated the wife of an excommunicated Catholic priest, who had become a Jewess. A Jewish physician was afterwards called in, who, along with the priest, denounced me to the authorities as having made somnambulistic diagnoses, etc. But the authorities refused to act in the matter. About this time Frau Anna Rothe came to my house, and I asked her control how the matter would turn out. The answer was, that a great number of Catholic "clerical spirits" were influencing the excommunicated priest to persecute me, in collusion with the doctor, because they did not wish that my efforts for the propagandism of animal magnetism and Spiritualism should be successful. The ideas of the Catholic Church had remained with these clericals even after death; but stronger powers would help me in this matter; and so it was! The exposure of the ex-priest and his medical accomplice was not at all bad, when they were turned back from the public law office, after they and those behind them had represented me in the press as already done for. There are, however, exceptions among the Catholic clergy, for I know some very agreeable, honourable, and high-minded ones among them; but even they have to be silent and obey. Moreover, in the States the Spiritualist Churches, or assemblies, whose announcements appear under the heading of churches, have for some time competed tolerably successfully with the Church. If we take up a Sunday paper, which contains the announcements of the churches, we can read the announcements of the Baptist, Christian, Christian Science, Congregational, Episcopal, Independent, Jewish, Lutheran, Methodist Episcopal, New Jerusalem, Presbyterian, Reformed Episcopal, Union, Unitarian, and Universalist Churches, and along with these a great number of Spiritualist meetings, in which for the most part religious discourses are given on ethics and philosophy in the theosophical sense as sketched above. Mrs. Pepper's "Aurora Grata Cathedral" in Brooklyn is crowded every Sunday, and at the close she always answers some of the letters which are presented in hundreds by the audience.

I do not think it necessary to give a detailed description of the four sittings with Miller in New York, for they resulted in nothing new, in addition to what I have already described, and what had already been fully described in the French journals, down to the smallest particular. I had previously purchased a curtain myself, and arranged it in a house which was quite strange to Mr. Miller; the sitters were all strangers to him, and yet the manifestations were still the same as ever. "Betsy" was exceedingly pleased to be able to talk with me again, and in English. It had been so hard for her to make herself understood in Europe, because she could only speak English. "Star Eagle" and "Dr. Benton" came afterwards, and many other spirits. White balls of muslinlike shining spiders' webs developed, even outside the cabinet, sank down from above, and quickly formed themselves into phantoms, among them those of old friends and acquaintances, one of whom embraced and kissed me, out of joy at seeing me again. The third sitting took place on Thirty-fourth Street, because the room in Eighty-fourth Street was too smoky, and I brought Herr Hermann Handrich, who placed an excellent article about it at the disposal of Dr. Bormann for *Die Uebersinnliche Welt,* Berlin. At this sitting a phantom materialised who called itself Katherine Bosshard, and spoke in Swiss dialect; she said that she came on Herr Handrich's account, whose family she knew well. He could not remember the name on that evening, but on the next day (Nov. 16th) I received a card from him in which he said: "Now I know who Katherine Bosshard was. Not a servant (he thought at first that it was perhaps some help in his parents' house in Switzerland), but the daughter of a Dr. Bosshard, who had charge of my dear little sister while our mother was on her deathbed." Also the already mentioned Frederika Hauffe, from Munich, came, and I had a long talk with her about everything that had happened in Europe; she spoke such lovely German that I was unwilling to see her go. Then Miller showed himself at the same time with the three Fox sisters, etc.

Professor Maier mentions in *Psychische Studien,* Leipzig, for December, 1906, page 755, according to the report in *L'Echo du Merveilleux,* that Betsy smelt strongly of tobacco, like Mr. Miller. I have often observed this with the phantoms which materialised with Miller. Even when I saw the phantom and Mr. Miller at the same time, it smelt strongly of tobacco, coffee, brandy, etc., according to what Mr. Miller had previously been taking. This is a singular phenomenon, but well known to experienced Spiritualists. It seems as though these vaporous beings took almost everything from their medium, of course including a great part of his ideas, so that, as I have already remarked, one cannot expect anything unadulteratedly original from them. The spirit comes for a moment from his own natural element into our earthly sphere, and du Prel is right when he says: "How the beings of the Beyond act *in their own element,* without being hindered by the corporeality either of themselves or of things around them, is a matter beyond our experience and comprehension."

On November 18th, 1906, Miller left again for San Francisco, while I remained in New York until December 8th. It had become very cold, so that I again became acquainted with snow and ice, and there was skating on the Hudson as the railroad took me along it to Albany. On the 9th I reached Chicago, and prepared my mind for the journey of three days and nights across the wastes of the central portion of North America. On the second day we crossed the now snow-clad Rocky Mountains, and on the third the Sierra Nevada, on which also the snow lay knee-deep. At last we were back in San Francisco, which I had quitted on August 4th, and was glad to see that in the meantime something had been done towards rebuilding the ruined city.

Building is going on everywhere, and trade is already very good. Mr. Miller has reopened his art and antiquities store on Post Street. But I was in search of warmer surroundings, and shortly before Christmas I reached Southern California once more, and took up my quarters in Hollywood, near the Mexican border, where the orange and citron trees ripen their fruit at that season. It is really beautiful there in winter, but in summer the everlasting sunshine makes one dull and takes away one's energy.

When I come to think again over the experiences of the last journey, I must admit that I have been drawn somewhat further in the direction of Theosophy. I am, however, still of the opinion that experimental Spiritualism forms the true basis for the certainty of a Future life. Crookes and Wallace, Zöllner, Fechner, Weber and Scheibner, Lombroso, Tamburini, Ascensi and many others would scarcely have come, but for experiment, to the conviction that Nature may be very much richer in facts than savants were aware, and have therefore freely admitted at least the facts of occultism. It must not indeed be assumed that they arrived at this recognition by themselves, that is, through their own carefully made observations. But once the experimental basis is established, the next step is to the higher knowledge of Theosophy, whose teachings must still remain within rational limits, and, where proofs are wanting, ought not to be clothed in the form of apodictic dogmas. Self-practice for one's own development appears to me to be the correct way.

As Professor Dr. Nagel pointed out in *Psychische Studien* (July, 1905, p. 428), even Professor Crookes, whose writings I have not at hand for reference here in the Wild West, tried to explain his experiences with Florence Cook on the animistic theory. According to this, it is possible for the subconsciousness, under certain peculiar circumstances, to project externally a form which can move about, and to clothe it with particles of matter, so that it appears for the moment in corporeal form. In the same way it explains all those apparently incomprehensible phenomena by the super-normal psychic powers of the medium. Gaston Mery also, in *L'Echo du Merveilleux,* proposes the explanation that the phantoms are formed by the will and fancy of the medium from the externalised odic layers.

With Miller I frequently saw—especially before he went into the cabinet—almost transparent phantoms of this kind, which also appear like substance externalised from the medium. But how is it, I ask myself, when I have seen the medium himself together with three separate phantoms, which had bodies as firm as his own, and two of them spoke English and one German with persons sitting in the circle, and whom the phantoms themselves had called to them while standing in front of the cabinet. And what are we to say when, on one of the three different photographs which I took with Miller, one of which was published, along with an article by Colonel de Rochas, in the journal, *"Je Sais Tout,"* of Paris, April 15, 1906, a phantom showed itself fully materialised, and having absolutely the appearance of my uncle, Theodor Neuberth, whom I had been very fond of when he was on earth, but of whom I had not thought for years, so that he was not in my mind, and I could not have telepathically influenced Mr. Miller? Moreover, I have heard these phantoms which appeared with Miller speak in the most diverse languages and dialects, whereas Miller, whom I have known for nearly four years, only speaks French and English.

Another question is, how far the knowledge and capacities of these momentarily formed human beings extends, and here I must confess that they do not go very far. For these beings, apparently transported back into the material world, as du Prel has justly said, do not show their *real* nature as regards mental qualities.

As regards what are called "revelations," I have received much better and deeper ones through other trance and speaking mediums. But these phenomena of transitory materialisation, as exhibited by Miller, have by far the higher value for the scientific researcher, and allow of more thorough investigation.

As I have already mentioned, I had many opportunities to meet Theosophists, and cannot deny that they present many elevated ideas; but it is difficult for a Christian, like myself, to reconcile myself to the difference between Christianity and Buddhism. Ernst Diestel has set forth this difference very clearly in the *Sphinx* (1895, p. 185) under the heading "Buddhism and Christianity." He says among other things: "And as in the Sermon on the Mount Jesus refers to Karma in many words and parables, so also in the woes pronounced on the Galilean towns (Matt. xi.), in the words as to the sin against the Holy Ghost, which cannot be forgiven (Matt. xii, 31-32); an account shall be given of every idle word. "By thy words thou shalt be justified and by thy words thou shalt be condemned" (Matt. xii, 37); in these words of Jesus the principle of divine justice is unconditionally laid down, and no grace can supersede it: a justice all the more terrible in that it implies a final, eternal separation on the Day of Judgment (Matt. xxv, 46); see also the Parable of the Wise and Foolish Virgins.

The inner law of this divine and merciless justice is enunciated by Christ in these words: "For unto everyone that hath shall be given, but from him that hath not shall be taken away even that which he hath" (Matt. xxv, 29).

We thus see that Karma has its place in Christianity also, but there is a very important difference. In Buddhism the principle of the divine law of Karma is carried out with definite consequences, but in Christianity these consequences are lacking. This arises from the fact that in Buddhism divine justice is an *impersonal, lifeless principle, in Christianity a personal, living God.* In the one, the principle is always the same, in rigid conformity with itself; in the other, we have the tenderly beating heart of a Heavenly Father, who leads his children, according to his own decree, through the sufferings of this world to their salvation; in the one case, there stretches over mankind, born from the dust, the vault of a heaven made rigid by eternal justice; in the other, this vault is broken by the word of heavenly grace: "Thy sins are forgiven thee."

I once asked the phantom, who called himself Dr. Benton, as to my former incarnations; he answered that he would ask "my soul," and tell me next time. I replied that this could soon be done; my soul was here. His answer was, no; that was an error; my soul was not here, but in the "spheres;" it was connected with my body by a cord, like a balloon, so that I, for instance, as my soul was developed, could not be drowned. This of course sounds very mystical, if not downright absurd. But the Alexandrian Neoplatonists, such as Plotinus and his teacher, Ammonius Saccas, asserted something similar. According to Plotinus, man has a double soul, a double Ego: the higher, which lives entirely in the supersensible world, and the lesser one, which is bound up with the body and its activities.* Saccas says on this point that the soul is partly on earth and thinks by means of the senses, and partly in the supersensible world without mediated thoughts.† This, moreover, is a very ancient idea. Whether it can be accepted as plausible in view of what I have set forth above, and in the present condition of our knowledge, I must leave the reader, who has followed me so far, to decide according to his own judgment.

On my return to California I had to stop four hours in Chicago, while awaiting the departure of the train for the Pacific Coast. It

---

*Plotinus, *Enneads* (the six groups, each consisting of nine books, of selections from his writings edited, with four supplements, by his pupil Porphyry), I, 1, 10; VI, 7, 5.

†Zeller: *Philosophie der Griechen*, III, 2, p. 456 (compare Du Prel, *Die Philosophie der Mystik*, Leipsic, Gunther, 1884, p. 448).

was Sunday, and I walked through the streets without any definite plan. At 135 Randolph Street I saw a sign: "Madame Seera, the Queen of Seers." In order to pass the time, I went in. Madame Seera calls herself Clairvoyant, Astrologist, and Palmist, and she possesses these talents in such a degree that she surpasses Madame de Thèbes, of Paris. She looked at me, and told me things which I had to admit were true, to my great astonishment. Then she examined the lines of my hand, and asked me to allow her to take an impression of them, for I had lines which are very rare, and promised to send me gratis a complete chart. (I have not found these lines of my hand mentioned, even in the important work on palmistry of Desbarolles, *Les Mystères de la Main,* Paris). I received the chart by post, very lengthily and carefully drawn out, and must acknowledge that no one has ever yet read my life so correctly as Madame Seera.

According to statements in her prospectus, she has read the hands of President Roosevelt, Governor Deneen of Illinois, President Harrison, J. Pierpont Morgan, John D. Rockefeller, Mme. Sarah Bernhardt, and many other celebrated personages. She claims to know nothing of spiritism! I have had a good deal to do with palmistry, or chiromancy, and have visited dozens of so-called palmists, mostly ignorant persons; Madame Seera and Madame de Thèbes prove that palmistry is true, but few understand it.

The hand is the chief officer of the soul. The Bible says: "Length of days is in her right hand, and in her left hand riches and honour" (Prov. iii, 16). "Thine hand shall find out all thine enemies: thy right hand shall find out those that hate thee" (Ps. xxi, 8). "And it shall be for a sign unto thee upon thine hand" (Ex. xiii, 9). "Behold I have graven thee upon the palms of my hand" (Isa. xlix, 16). "In the hands of all men God hath placed some sign by which they know their work" (Book of Job). Fourteen hundred and thirty-three times does the Bible speak of the human hand. Thus we find that palmistry is in perfect harmony with the Bible.

Madame Seera gives the following remarkable account of the temple in which she studied it:

"Close to the ancient city of Benares, situated upon a beautiful hill, in the midst of solitude and loneliness, is a cave temple, which has been owned and protected by the Joshi Priests, who have practised palmistry in all the generations from 1000 B.C. to the present day.

"In this temple, musty with years and mysticism, are hidden invaluable books on palmistry, written on silver and gold plates. There are three maps of the hand on human skin, written in a bright red colour which age and sun cannot obliterate.

"They are supposed to have been written on human skin for preservation, as they have been preserved in the same manner as the mummies. They are finely illustrated, containing great information on palmistry, which has been a perfected science with the Hindus from time immemorial. The dates of two of these hands are unknown, but one shows 1000 B.C.

"This cave is the most sacred and holy spot to the Hindus, the great men of India, who have astonished the world with their psychic power, having gained their knowledge at this temple. Not only the Hindus themselves, but the most celebrated palmists in Europe, such as the well-known Cheiro and others, have perfected their knowledge in this temple."

Madame Seera gives an honest and truthful delineation of future events. Many have already come true. For instance, she gives the following as having already come to pass:

"President Roosevelt's nomination, accidents in July and October, his miraculous escape from death, and his overwhelming victory were forecast through a horoscope published in the Chicago *Inter-Ocean*.

"The great danger which threatened the Czar of Russia; the great disasters on land and sea, were forecast in a horoscope cast for Alexis, heir to the Imperial throne of Russia, by request for the Chicago *Evening American* and published August 27, 1904.

"The accident to King Edward VII. of England, which occurred November 15, 1905, was forecast by Madame Seera in an astrological horoscope, published June 16, 1905, in the Chicago *Inter-Ocean*.

"The great disaster of San Francisco was also forecast by Mme. Seera on February 4, 1905, in the *Evening Post*.

X.

Before I finally left the shores of the Pacific Ocean, in order, as already stated, to reside in the Eastern States, I resolved to undertake the long planned voyage to the Hawaiian Islands, Japan, China, and the Philippines.

On April 17, 1907, for the last time for the present, I went on board the steamer at Port Los Angeles for San Francisco, had a short talk with Mr. Miller, who complained of pains in his heart, and on April 23 went on board the steamship "Korea" of the Pacific Mail Steamship Company. The "Korea" is only of 12,000 tons, but she is one of the best boats that cross the Pacific. We took seventeen days to get to Yokohama, for the steamers of this line call at Honolulu, and therefore take a somewhat southerly course; but I had rather travel for seventeen days on the sea than three days in a train. These steamers have not the almost too stately sumptuousness of the Norddeutscher

Lloyd and Hamburg-American lines, and unfortunately there is no music on board, but they are very good, and faultless as regards lighting and bathrooms. The service is performed by Chinamen, who are very different from the American waiters, each of whom acts as though he were a baron. The after-deck is used only by the Chinese, who play all day long—a sort of dominoes, dice, and cards—even a roulette was to be seen. Dirty, half-naked, smelling of opium, they crouch in a circle, and eat their rice, meat, etc., out of a common dish with sticks.

On the sixth day we reached Oahu, Hawaiian Islands, and stopped for eight hours at Honolulu. The cocoanut and sago palms, the Royal Palm, rice, sugar, etc., grow there. The Moana Hotel, situated right by the sea, buried in tropical vegetation, brought me nearer to the Nirvana of Buddhism. Black-brown Kanakas, the aborigines of the Hawaiian Islands, dived after coins like the South Italians at Castellamare on the Gulf of Naples, and I stood in wonder in the Aquarium, which contains fishes of the Southern Seas in quite incredible variety of forms and colours. An ichthyologist would have a good time here. But the tropical sun burnt hotly, and I was quite ready to leave these wonderful islands. The distance from San Francisco to Honolulu is 2100 miles, and from Honolulu to Yokohama 3445 miles. On May 3 we passed the 180th degree of longitude, where we skip a whole day, and two days before we sighted the Japanese coast a cyclone gripped us, and Æolus and Neptune fought hard with each other. At night on May 9th we reached Yokohama, and on the 10th, after a medical examination, we went ashore in the Land of the Chrysanthemum, cherry-blossom, and lotus flowers.

I could easily write a book about my impressions of travel in Japan and China, but these would not be suited to the compass of the present little work, which is mainly concerned with metaphysical subjects, and I must therefore be brief.

On landing in Japan the traveller is beset by a lot of rickshaws, small two-wheeled carriages which are drawn by a running Japanese; horses are not used, except for military purposes. In Japan people do everything themselves, and as the Japanese live almost entirely on rice, fish, and vegetables, there are very few cattle, practically no sheep or swine, and therefore little manure except human excrement, the smell of which is very offensive to travellers. Those who know this eat no raw fruit, such as strawberries, etc. Every spot of ground is planted with rice, tea, wheat, and barley, even on the hills, for the 49,700,000 (nearly) inhabitants have to make all the use they can of the 162,372 square miles of land, most of it mountainous, in order to live.

Yokohama is the second treaty port of Japan, and was opened to foreign trade in July, 1859. The scenery around is hilly and pleasing, and on clear days the snow-crowned summit and graceful outlines of Fuji-san are most distinctly visible. Beyond the plain on which the town is built rises a sort of semi-circle of low hills called The Bluff, which is thickly dotted with handsome foreign villas and dwelling houses in various styles of architecture, all standing in pretty gardens. During my stay at Yokohama I visited the porcelain manufacturers, and at one of them, Kawamoto's, Egg-shell Porcelain Manufacturer, 18 Honcho, I had a porcelain service made with figures of warriors in old Japanese armour. I then visited the cloisonné, lacquer, wood-carving and bronze exhibits. I was also present at a tea ceremonial. The Japanese have no furniture; people sit on straw mats, and a girl, with slow, tripping steps, brings in tea and cakes, kneels down in front of the guests and places the tea and cakes in front of each with continual nodding of her head. I made acquaintance with some new fruits there; the sweet mango fruit, the mangosteen, the Lychee, and the Papaia. The cold North knows nothing of these fruits of the Orient.

Except at the Grand Hôtel, Yokohama, which charges American prices, everything in Japan costs about half as much as in the United States; but in this hotel one receives the best attention.

In about half an hour by railroad from Yokohama we reach Kamakura, with the forty-nine feet high bronze statue of the Buddha—the Dai-Butsu—then the Sacred Island, opposite to Enoshima, by a two-wheeled jinrikisha or rickshaw drawn by a running Japanese. In the capital, Tokio, I admired the wonderful wisterias, with their pendent masses of blue flowers. Tokio has about 1,819,000 inhabitants, and

I have never in any country seen such an abundance of children as in Japan. In parts of Tokio there are beautiful broad avenues, and in the neighbourhood is the palace of the Mikado, standing on an eminence, surrounded by a stone wall and water, with many modern European buildings. I saw many soldiers, the infantry resembling the German and the cavalry the French, and museums containing trophies from the Russo-Japanese war. The Imperial Hôtel meets European and American requirements fairly well.

I afterwards went into the interior, to Miyanoshita. The road to this place is not unlike the Swiss country roads, with high mountains, deep valleys, and noisy brooks. At the Fujiya Hôtel there one finds every comfort. In a chair carried by four Japanese bearers I made an excursion to the Hakone Lake, passing the Ojigoku, a smoking volcano, like that in the Yellowstone Park, Wyoming. On May 18 I left the Fujiya Hôtel to go to Nagoya; during the journey one sees for hours the snow-clad Fujiyama (12,365 feet high). This holy mountain with its white top, surrounded by green meadows, affords a lovely prospect. In

Nagoya, during the three days of my stay, I did not see a single European. The Temple of Go Hyaku Rakan there contains 500 different statues of Buddha. Every sculptor thinks that his own is the only correct looking one; I also saw there the manufacture of cloisonné, that wonderful silver work executed on copper. In the Misonoza Theatre I saw the Japanese Feast of Flowers represented; the Flower-Dance of the Geishas is unique, but the Japanese have no notion of music. On wooden drums and a kind of guitar they make a noise that one would gladly run away from. As the Japanese have no furniture, the spectators sit in square groups of four on straw mats, in the middle of which stand the tea-urn and smoking utensils.

From Nagoya I passed through miles of bamboo forest to Kyoto, and put up at the Kyoto Hotel. This city is prettily situated, and is divided into two halves by the Kamo River. Kyoto is celebrated for its dancing girls. During my visit I was present at a Japanese dinner at one of the most exclusive tea-houses, with Geishas and dancing girls in attendance. There were ten of us, and as we ought to have taken off our shoes, which I did not wish to do, our shoes were covered with linen over-shoes, and we were shown into a room, where we had to sit on straw mats with our legs crossed under us, which is not so easy to manage. Little Geisha girls then brought us a little square table, a foot high, with fish in lacquered wooden trays, unknown kinds of vegetables in similar trays, Japanese candy, and saki (rice spirit). Everything was very neat and clean, but we could not eat fish and vegetables in lacquered trays. Then a Geisha in her pretty costume sat down before each guest in order to serve him. These twelve to fourteen year old Geishas are very inquisitive. They freely handled each guest, took off his rings and jewelry and bedecked themselves with them. They had little mirrors and cosmetics in their kimonos (Japanese robes). But one easily permits such liberties from such charming creatures.

I visited the great Shinto shrines, the Yakasa Pagoda, the Dai-Butzu, the San-ju-san-gen-do Temple with its thousand images of Kwannon, God of Mercy. Each has several heads and several arms, so that they can grant all manner of wishes. Then there is the Higashi Hongwanji Temple with an enormous rope made of women's hair, to which 10,000 women are said to have given their hair, so that it could be used for the erection of the pillars. I have never yet seen any country in which the people are so contented as they are in Japan; healthy, strong, rosy cheeked, frugal, and always cheerful. My rickshaw-boy, my human horse, was named Mino. Wherever he took me, he ran along at a smart trot, always smiling cheerfully, waiting patiently when required, and laughing whenever he turned to look back at me; and when on the last day I gave him the travelling-cap I had brought from London, he put it on instead of his straw hat, and ran still more merrily through the streets, which at most were only seven feet wide.

From Kyoto I made a day's trip to Nara, which made the most lasting impression upon me, with the exception of Nikko, which I saw afterwards. The wonderful, primeval forest roads, where you drive between stone pillars, each dedicated to the memory of a deceased person, with shrines and temples in between, hundreds of tame deer, which throng around and eat out of your hand, then the Japanese in their charming costumes, the Shinto Temples, where

I witnessed the sacred dance of young Shinto priestesses, the holy horse, which awaits the God who will ride on him to the sanctuaries which are consecrated to himself, etc. This wonderful natural beauty, these centuries-old cedars, make a deep impression on the visitor.

From Nara I went to Kobe, the second largest export centre in Japan. I stopped at the Oriental Hotel. Kobe is the place where the foreigners make most of their purchases. Silks, cloisonné enamel, lacquered work, ivory, and silver articles are all nearly three times cheaper than in the United States, which levy a customs duty of 30 to 60 per cent. on these goods.

I will here speak of Nikko, though I did not visit it until after my return from China. Its shady woods, its extensive groves and lofty avenues, its religious air, make Nikko an ideal place for the dreamer. Percival Lowell* says:

"At the farther end rises a building, the like of which for richness of effect you have probably never beheld nor even imagined. In front of you a flight of white stone steps leads up to a terrace whose parapet, also of stone, is dia-

---

The Soul of the Far East, Boston and New York, Houghton, Mifflin & Co., 1888.

pered for half its height and open lattice work the rest. This piazza gives entrance to a building or set of buildings whose every detail challenges the eye. Twelve pillars of snow-white wood sheathed in part with bronze, arranged in four rows, make, as it were, the bones of the structure. The space between the centre columns lies open. The other triplets are webbed in the middle, and connected on the sides and front by grilles of wood and bronze, forming on the outside a couple of embrasures on either hand the entrance, in which stand the guardian Nio, two colossal demons, Gog and Magog. Instead of capitals, a frieze, bristling with Chinese lions, protects the top of the pillars. Above this, in place of entablature, rise tier upon tier of decoration, each tier projecting beyond the one beneath, and the topmost of all terminating in a balcony which encircles the whole second story. The parapet of this balcony is one mass of ornament, and its cornice another row of lions, brown instead of white. The second story is no less crowded with carving. Twelve pillars make its ribs, the spaces between being filled with elaborate woodwork, while on top more friezes, more cornices, clustered with excrescences of all colours and kinds, and guarded by lions innumerable. To begin to tell the details of so multifacetted a gem were artistically impossible. It is a jewel of a thousand rays, yet whose beauties blend into one, as the prismatic tints combine to white. And then, after the first dazzle of admiration, when the spirit of curiosity urges you to penetrate the centre aisle, lo and behold, it is but a gate! The dupe of unexpected splendour, you have been paying court to the means of approach. It is only a portal after all. For as you pass through you catch a glimpse of a building beyond more gorgeous still. Like in general to the first, unlike it in detail, resembling it only as the mistress may the maid. But who shall convince of charm by enumerating the feature of a face! From the tiles of its terrace to the encrusted gables that drape it as with some rich bejeweled mantle, falling about it in the most graceful of folds, it is the very Eastern Princess of a building, standing in the majesty of her court to give you audience.

A pebbly path, a low flight of stone steps, a pause to leave your shoes without the sill, and you tread in the twilight of reverence upon the moss-like mats within. The richness of its outer ornament, so impressive at first, is, you discover, but prelude to the lavish luxury of its interior. Lacquer, bronze, pigments, deck its ceiling and its sides in such profusion that it seems to you as if art had expanded in the congenial atmosphere into a tropical luxuriance of decoration, and grew here as naturally on temples as in the jungle creepers do on trees.

The world-famous temples of Nikko are the burial places of the first and third Shoguns of the Tokugawa line of the seventeenth century. The Red Lacquer Sacred Bridge, these avenues of gigantic Cryptomerias, these wonderful temples in the midst of primeval forests, this dream-wealth of Nature, make Nikko the most attractive place in Japan. I stayed at the Nikko Hotel, and made an excursion with sedan-chairs to Lake Chuzenji—a dream-place. I saw the Sacred Horse again in Nikko, and again witnessed the sacred dance of the Shinto priestesses.

An intimate friend of mine in Los Angeles, a colonel, who travelled in Japan in 1897, told me that he had observed the remains of Phallus-worship in Japan. As I could not discover anything of such worship, in spite of repeated inquiries, I asked him where he had seen it. His reply was as follows:

"In Nikko, going from the red bridge up the road following the river, and about 500 yards from the bridge, is a shrine standing on wooden piers, a simple, barn-like structure. In 1897, I saw under the shrine, piled up quite indiscriminately, about fifty phalli carved out of stone, of different sizes, from normal to heroic. Outside the shrine are a lot of stone 'lanterns' (so-called), may be ten of them, standing, with pedestal, about four feet high. Before the phallic worship was suppressed—say in 1878—each 'lantern' contained one of these stone carvings, placed upright, and the women worshipped there. As I examined the ground near by, I noticed that the grass was worn away in front of some of the lanterns, as though by the tread of many feet, leading to the belief that in the darkness of night women still worship there. At the time of the suppression, the emblems were discarded and thrown under the shrine. We understood that everywhere in Japan these phallic emblems were in use formerly. This particular shrine was Buddhist."

I am sorry to say that I was not able to have any metapsychical experiences in Japan. As regards the religious belief of the Japanese, Mime Inness contributed the following very interesting article to the *"Banner of Light"* for February 24, 1906:

KARMA AND SHINTOISM IN JAPAN.

When Admiral Togo, after his successive victories, took occasion to thank, in the most formal way, the spirits of the dead for their assistance in the war in which they had lain down their earthly lives, to most Americans it seemed an act of Eastern barbarism, strangely injected into modern life.

How could a great naval captain like Togo be so superstitious, so ignorant?

It is, however, not strange that one reared, as is every Japanese, in the Shinto philosophy, should take occasion, as a thank offering, to recognize one of the most prevalent of Japanese ideas.

The Japanese is reared not only upon the doctrine of Shinto, which is peculiar to his people, but the Buddhistic doctrines of pre-existence and Karma enter equally into the make-up of his religious life. We in the West have but an indistinct idea of pre-existence. Theosophists maintain the doctrine, but the ordinary Christian, especially those reared in Calvinism, have spent all their religious lives in an effort to save their own individual souls from a hereafter which is represented to be so horrible that escape from it is the one "consummation devoutly to be wished."

But the Oriental philosophy takes care of all this sort of thing in an entirely different way, a way which is almost inexplicable to the self-seeking Occidental.

"In the first place," says the Jap, "my own soul is not a single thing. It is a term of reproach to me when one tells me derisively, 'I can see that you have but one soul.' My soul cannot exist for an eternity hereafter unless it has already existed for an eternity before this life.

"Eternity is an endless thing. Nothing can be endless if it have a beginning. The Occidental talks of a life in the future which has no end. Then it can have had no beginning; for an endless thing with one end is endless. I must, therefore, have existed from all eternity if I am to live to all eternity.

"Therefore, I know that my soul, in its pre-existent states, has passed through many earth-lives, has had all the experiences which those pre-existing lives imply. It is not, cannot be, a single thing, one soul. It is a composite of all the experiences of all past eternities through which it has lived. In me to-day exist consciously the souls of all my kindred by heredity, and no small part of those other lives with which I have lived and by contact have partaken of. Hence, my ancestors, being those to whom I owe, not my existence alone, but all those attributes which make my soul what it is, are certainly worthy of my highest regard and worship.

"Not only this" (and here comes in the Spiritualistic idea), "but these ancestors, as is natural, take in me and my living, the deepest interest. They surround my daily pathway, seeking in every way they can to enhance for me the good and to ward off the bad. What is more natural for the parent who dies than to maintain his interest in his child? You western Christians believe in a heaven to which a dying father goes and shuts from his knowledge everything in which, two minutes before he breathed his last, he was most deeply concerned; or, if you believe that he still has knowledge of the lives of his children, he is yet powerless to affect those lives for good or ill. This is still worse than total ignorance. For what is more devilish, what could be a greater Hell, than to be compelled to sit supinely by and see the tortures of a child and be powerless to aid? We know better than this. When we die and slough off the flesh, we do not change. We still love, and love implies aid. We still hover near and help to bear the burden or share the joy of our children, making it greater by the sharing.

"So, while we worship our ancestors, we know they are worthy of worship. Do you Occidentals still wish an angry God to punish sin? He does punish it, not as one angry, but as one who is just. Sin is not like the naughtiness of a child, to be punished by a slipper. It is a breaking of God's laws, which breaking always bears its own consequences. If I violate the law of gravitation and walk off the roof of the house, I fall, not as a punishment for violating the law, but because a violation of the law entails its own consequences.

"So if I do wrong, I suffer. No pardon, no repentance, avails to wash away the sin. It entails its own punishment, leaves forever its own scar. Thereby I am taught not to sin.

"But the consequence of my violation of God's law is that the scar remains. I may not work out my own redemption, until death has seized me. The consequences of that wrong go on just the same, and when next my undying soul seeks physical embodiment, the stain of my sin is still on it, the law is still operative and justice still demands of me the working out of my own redemption. The 'sins of the father are visited upon the children' is true, not as a punishment, but as a simple, just working-out of the rule of the law. This is Karma. Evil in my life I know is just, not for what I have done in this embodiment, but for what I did in another body. Joy is mine, not always for my own merits, but for the good I did when here before. Is not this justice? Is not this right? Does not this explain why life is as it is? Is not this a good and sufficient reason for my ancestor worship?"

This is why the Japanese see so little that is attractive in Christianity. This is why they are Spiritualists. This is why Shintoism and Buddhism are to them the living forces that they are.

This is why this life, seeming such a trifling part of the real life, is with so little hesitation thrown away by a Japanese in battling for a good cause.

If Western civilization could take a leaf from the book of the little yellow men of the islands, creeds might suffer, but the real life of Christ would be more purely lived, and then indeed would "death be swallowed up in victory," being no longer the "King of Terrors."

MIME INNESS.

At Kobe I embarked in the "America Maru," a Japanese steamer with an English captain, Philip Going, one of the seven worthiest of men, and a Japanese crew and Chinese servants, in order to go through the Inland Sea to Nagasaki. The Inland Sea is universally conceded to be the most magnificent sheet of water in the world, with a length of about 240 miles. The channel in places is so narrow that it will hardly permit the passing of two ships, and from the time the steamer enters it through the Straits of Akashi until she passes out through the Straits of Shimonoseki it is one gorgeous panorama. The sea is studded with islands of every conceivable shape and size, from the barren rock standing up alone in its grandeur to large islands artificially terraced from the water's edge to the summit, and all under the highest cultivation. Scene succeeds scene, picture follows picture, with such surprising rapidity that one can scarcely spare time for meals. Unlike most parts of Japan the islands in this sea are lightly wooded. There is an unrivalled view hereabouts.

The clear, shallow water of this famous sea, picturesquely dotted with beautiful little islands —decked with shrines and miniature temples— forms as near an approach to Fairyland as can be expected in a matter of fact world. A Fairyland, indeed, of islands and temples and trees, possessed of a charm which even the picturesque Lafcadio Hearn's polished language failed to fitly describe. Here is a chance, if taken by easy stages, criss-crossing from island to island, to see Japan in its pristine beauty. There are islands here where the foot of the white man has never rested.

The boat takes twenty-eight hours to reach Nagasaki. After passing Shimonoseki the boat passes through the Tsushima Straits, where Togo annihilated the Russian fleet, and comes to Nagasaki, with its wonderful harbour and historical associations. Just in front of the city is the island of Deshima, noted as being the scene of martyrdom of so many Christians. Not far inland are the historic castle of Kumamoto, and Kagoshima, the capital of Satsuma province. At Nagasaki and Kagoshima one can buy specimens of the genuine old Satsuma porcelain, so prized by collectors.

XI.

On May 27, 1907, we began our voyage through the Eastern Sea and South China Sea to Manila, the capital of the Philippines. The voyage lasted three and a half days, and the discomforts of this journey will never be forgotten. For five years I lived in an almost tropical climate in Southern California, but there the nights are cool, while in this journey there was no cessation of the heat. All day long we were under a fiery tropical sun, and at night we slept on deck. On the 28th the mountains of Formosa rose above the horizon, and on the 30th the lighthouse at Luzon came into view.

Manila is an old Spanish city, very hot in spite of the tropical vegetation of all kinds, among which the mindanao tree with its dark red flowers pleased me the most. I made an excursion of about two hours to the American barracks, where the heat was unbearable. The natives still live in their straw huts, erected on four piles, and use boats made of a hollowed-out tree trunk. At the "Germinal" cigar factory, which employs 1500 workmen, the very amiable manager explained to me all that was worth knowing about the manufacture of tobacco, and gave besides to each one of our party of ten persons a box of choice Manila cigars.

The Philippines are the sore spot of the United States; they are said to have cost up to now 400 million dollars for development, and bring very little in. The principal articles of commerce are hemp, sugar, tobacco, cigars, and coffee. They are extremely fruitful, but not yet two per cent. of their area is developed. White men cannot work there, and the natives are too lazy. What is to be done with the Philippines is now being much discussed in the American papers. They can be reached by a warship from Japan in three and a half days, while the distance from San Francisco is twenty-eight days. I have nothing to do with politics, but I cannot help thinking that Japan will some day have the Philippines. The *Japan Advertiser,* of Yokohama, published the following on June 21, 1907:

THE DISPOSAL OF THE PHILIPPINES.

SHOULD THEY BE GIVEN TO JAPAN?

The *Times* New York correspondent in a recent telegram remarks:

There is no episode in the history of their country which Americans now look back upon with more regret than the war with Spain. The newspapers do not often care to give expression to this feeling, but it is practically universal from the Atlantic to the Pacific. Universal also is the belief that the Philippines are the biggest white elephant with which the country has ever been burdened, and that the islands will never be anything more than a burden. If they could be handed over to Japan or handed back to Spain without loss of national dignity it would be done. This, of course, is impossible, but the heartfelt regret of the American people for the Spanish adventure can be and is manifested by the offer of friendship to Spain, which it is hoped Spain will accept.

Writing on this subject in the *Contemporary Review*, Mr. John Foreman contends that the ultimate destiny of the Philippine Islands "may be voluntary or compulsory union with Japan. If ever the cloud appearing on the political horizon should point to that contingency, America could well save her national dignity by conceding independence before the appointed time, as an act of grace."

On June 2, still in the "American Maru," I left Manila and in forty-two hours arrived at Hongkong in China. Black clouds collected into masses, and a deluge of rain came down on the ship, but it brought no coolness with it. The Southern Cross could be seen at night, and on the morning of the third day the steamer lay in the wondrously beautiful harbour of Victoria, Hongkong.

Hongkong is one of the finest harbours of the world, and is also a free port—no customs duties, no unpleasant medical examination. England has done great things here. In the British possessions, such as Vancouver and Hongkong, the first things to strike one are the colossal and massive public buildings. Ships from all over the world lie in the harbour. The Peak rises in terraces behind the narrow coast strip, and wonderfully beautiful is the road leading up to the summit, 2000 feet high. There is a splendid view from here over the harbour, with its countless ships, and little islands, and even at this elevation tropical plants grow. Indian and Chinese silk is the principle article of commerce, and is mostly in the hands of Indians; the military and police forces also consist of Indians, with black frizzled beards and wearing turbans. Sedan chairs and rickshaws are generally used here. One of the things that impressed me most was the remarkable Parsee cemetery. There are 10,000 Europeans and about 200,000 Chinese dwelling in Hongkong, and the population includes Turks, Mahometans, Hindoos, Javanese, Japanese, Malays, Parsees, Cingalese, Portuguese, and other races. I stopped at the King Edward Hotel, a gigantic building.

From Hongkong I made an excursion by the steamship "Kinshan" of the Hongkong, Canton and Macao Steamboat Company, to Canton. The voyage took about eight hours, up the Pearl River, and here I saw for the first time a real Chinese city.

Canton has about three million inhabitants; countless sampans (small flat-bottomed boats) lie in the river, on which about 200,000 people live, marry, and die, and some of them never set foot on firm ground. We went through the city in carrying-chairs, and the smell of the place was horrible.

All the trade is carried on in the streets, which are only about seven feet wide, so that we were often unable to get either forward or backward. I visited the Temple of Five Hundred Genii, the Water Clock, the Temple of Horrors with its swarms of beggars and fortune-tellers. In this temple Chinese tortures are represented by means of figures. Nothing worse was ever invented by the mediæval Inquisitors. One sees the delinquents thrown naked into boiling oil, or pinned down to the ground with an iron fork. Other figures show the skin being torn from the living body of the condemned man, etc. I then visited the execution ground, a narrow, dreary, dirty spot in the middle of the city. The executioneer, a tall, half-naked Chinaman, showed me the axe with which he had only five days before beheaded a condemned man. A dead man's skull lay under one stone, and a jawbone full of teeth under another. A place full of horrors! I tried in vain to take this executioner with my kodak; he made off as soon as I tried to photograph him. It is an interesting fact that the Chinese will not allow themselves to be photographed; even the bearers of our chairs turned away when we pointed the camera at them. Every Chinese cherishes the hope that he will some day be rich, and does not wish to be reminded of his former poverty.*

Canton is the place for the purchase of silk, ivory, linen, and jade (a green stone, only found in China and Burma). Between the temples one sees the panorama of the open shops, streets of silk and jade and jewelers' shops; weavers' dens and gold-beaters' caves; shoe shops, cabinet shops, meat and cook shops on either side. Unknown cookery simmers, sputters and scents the air. Dried ducks hang by half-yard-long necks, and a queer flat bit of dried meat declares itself by the long, thin tail curled like a grape tendril, to be the rat. The rat is in the market everywhere, alive in cages, fresh or dried on

---

*Is there not another and an occult reason for this? When we remember that one of the processes of witchcraft, known in France as envoûtement, consists in sticking pins into an image of the person intended to be harmed, it is evident that there is a widespread belief that the possession of the portrait confers a formidable power over the person himself.—(Translator's Note.)

meat-shop counters, and dried ones are often bought as souvenirs of a day in Canton and proof of the often-denied rat story. Theatres are many; shops of theatrical wardrobes are endless in one quarter; dealers in old costumes abound, and there are pawn shops and curio shops without end.

The Chinese are fanatical, and I was glad to be back again on the "Kinshan," which started on her return voyage to Hongkong at night, with the Southern Cross still shining above us.

On June 11 I re-embarked in the "America Maru," and in fifty-three hours reached Shanghai, passing between the Chinese coast and the west side of Formosa, and into the Yellow Sea, with its numerous islands and countless fishing boats; a thick bank of fog forced us to stop for an hour before we reached Woosung. Here the steamer stopped, and a steam launch took the passengers off and conveyed them up the Yangtse-Kiang River to Shanghai in an hour and a half. The nearer we got to Shanghai, the more interesting the prospect became. Warships from all over the world lie here, always ready for attack.

These powerful fleets of England, Germany,

France, America, and Japan form an imposing sight, but they are necessary on account of the fanaticism of the Chinese people. Shanghai is called the Paris of the East, and the European portions of the city are very pretty, the German club-house being especially noticeable. I stayed at the Astor House, which can be well recommended. Generally speaking, an epicure should not come to China! In Shanghai there are English, American, and French colonies, each of which has its own police force.

During a carriage excursion into the neighbouring country, I saw dozens of coffins, wrapped about with straw, standing in the fields. The Chinese inject a fluid into the bodies of the dead, which preserves them for a long time, and after a year they put stones around the coffin and leave the dead man on his own former property.

I left again on the 15th of June, crossed the Yellow Sea, and came again to Nagasaki on the 17th. A hundred and eighty men of the crew had their pulses examined for fever, and we first-class passengers were thoroughly inspected; this is always done in Japanese ports. Then we went through the beautiful Inland Sea to

Kobe, and after having been forced by a typhoon to anchor for eight hours in Osaka Bay, we once more arrived at Yokohama, where I left the "America Maru" with her most amiable captain.

Margaret MacLean has recently published a little book, *Chinese Ladies at Home* (Methodist Publishing House, Tokio, 1906), in which she writes as follows:

"Taking it on the whole, I do not like the Chinese, and loathe the country, but could not help feeling sorry for the tremendous hold superstition has on them. The evil spirit is a terrible creature. A creature constantly needing to be outwitted; fortunately, he is easily deceived. It always puzzled me that the evil spirit's influence could be deemed so powerful when he is so easily deceived. Spirit-walls are built in front of doors. The evil one can see, or at least knows, that the door is there, but can have no knowledge of the wall that protects it, for as he can go only in straight lines he attempts to enter the door and goes bang up against the wall and shoots off down the street; again, if he tries to slide down the ridge of the roof he is shot into the air by the ridge being curved upward. It would seem as though he were a shuttlecock, which must constantly be kept moving, or disaster will come. A boy will wear an earring so that the evil spirit will think he is a girl and not worth venting his evil influence upon. At a certain time, New Year, I think, the evil spirit can get beyond the spirit-wall to the very door of the house, but there hangs a mirror in which he sees his ugly self, and thinking it is another evil spirit, and that he will be caught trespassing, he hurries away. Fire-crackers and noise will also frighten him, and as noise is cheap it is plentifully used. Judging from the population of the country the temples are not much frequented by worshippers—notice I say worshippers, for they are much frequented by beggars, and buyers and sellers, and barbers. I could see now what Jesus did when He went into the Temple and cast out all those that sold and bought. The temples are dirty, untidy, and full of rubbish. The gods are sometimes out of repair.

"A god out-at-elbows, so to speak, or looking seedy, cannot inspire high thoughts, but he is all the people have to turn to and the fact that they turn to him even in his painfully made-by-men condition, shows their hearts are longing for something beyond this world and greater than themselves.

"During my entire visit to China I never wished to compare the Chinese to the Japanese; to me they seemed so totally different. Indeed, the Chinese in many ways could be compared to us more correctly than to the Japanese. The manner of the Chinese has more of our brusqueness than it has the graciousness of the Japanese. Their houses, too, are so totally different from those of their island neighbours that comparisons can not be made, although differences can be stated, and so with the temples. When it is said that they are both heathen, and both have many gods in common, then the resemblance ends. In a Japanese temple there is a sacred stillness that in itself is beneficial, and every place is clean. If cleanliness be next to godliness, then the Chinese temples are far, far from godliness. The noises of buyers and sellers arguing the price, the noise of hawkers, the din of the general uproar is inappropriate, to say the least.

"The 'Temple of the Eight Hundred Gods' seemed not so much a temple as a repository for gods. All the temples I saw needed repairing, but were neglected except this one, whose needs were receiving attention. Most of the gods in this temple had kindly benevolent countenances, making it a much pleasanter place to visit. The god of fire had a bright red face and three eyes—the third being in his forehead and at right angles to the other two. Most of the peculiar things about the gods have a reason, so when I noticed one with a black hand I inquired. Very often these inquiries reveal interesting history, but this time the answer was that he was being repaired and when finished the hand would be a more natural colour for that divinity. The entrance to this temple was a perfect circle built of stone beautifully carved. In China, the outside walls of temples are usually painted pink, or yellow, so wherever those coloured walls are seen a temple is indicated, although there may be temples with walls unpainted.

"In all their Guild Houses they have a temple, but these cannot be classed as public temples. The only Guild House I was in was the Shansi Bankers' Guild House in Shanghai, which is said to be the finest specimen of Chinese architecture in that city. It is certainly very beautiful. The courtyards, made of stone, and with octagonal gates, make excellent photographs. When one sees these typical Chinese doorways for the first time, one exclaims 'How Oriental!' and they continue to strike one as genuinely picturesque. Entering the reception hall, with its tables, chairs, scrolls, and opium couches, one finds everything clean. Now, a clean place is so rare that it is worthy of comment. As this is a bankers' guild, the god of wealth occupies a prominent place along with his ministers, 'Invite Riches' and 'Gain Market.' The shrine is red lacquered, touched here and there with gold, and all the accessories for temple worship are of the finest and kept in perfect condition.

"Ancestral worship is the basis of Chinese religious belief. The spirits that pass after death into the other world have necessities, and want comforts; and so the faithful descendants of the dead have need to send them houses, boats, clothing, sedan chairs, and money. It is a make-believe offering, for the luxuries bestowed upon the spirits are in the form of paper models, or emblems. These paper things are burnt and their substance floats away in smoke, to the grateful acceptance of the expectant dead. That which a Chinaman desires, above all else, is a son to keep green his memory and attend to his wants in the next world; and, before even these, to give his body an appropriate burial. This service is not all unselfish on the part of the son, for Ancestral worship includes the idea that if the son be unfaithful to his father calamity will befall him.

"China is awakening to her situation. We fear the yellow peril. China fears the white peril. A cartoon published in a Chinese paper shows why they fear the white peril. In the north is the Russian bear; in the centre the English bull-dog; in the south-east the Yankee eagle; in the south the French frog; while about Formosa is Japan's lasso; and around Shangtung are a line of German sausages."

XIII.

On June 29, 1907, I left Japan by the steamship "Siberia" of the Pacific Mail, and on July 8 reached Honolulu, and on the 14th San Francisco, after having had two Fourths of July, as the 180th degree of longitude was passed on that day.

When I arrived at San Francisco the city was looking dismal; a car strike of three months' duration had paralyzed all business, so that Mr. Miller expressed the intention of selling out his business and going to New York or Paris; but I went on after a fortnight to Chicago and thence to Lily Dale, to recuperate in the woods of that charming spot from the exertions of my journey in the Orient, and to have some further occult experiences.

This time I met Mr. W. J. Colville there, whose new book, *Universal Spiritualism* (New York, R. F. Fenno & Company), had just appeared. I have never heard so distinguished a teacher of Spiritualism as he is. Mrs. Richmond, Mr. Oscar A. Edgerly, Mr. J. Clegg Wright, are excellent speakers, but they do not come up to Mr. Colville. His book, to which I have just referred, is excellent, even though I regret to have to say that he has almost entirely passed over the German spiritualist literature, as represented by such men as Dr. Carl du Prel and Baron Hellenbach, who are hardly surpassed by any writers in the world.

There were also some good psychometrists at Lily Dale, such as Georgia Gladys Cooley, Mrs. Susanne Harris, etc. It would seem as though it was necessary for these psychics to have a large circle around them, in order to give good tests, for in private sittings they were not so reliable as in public ones at which dozens of sitters were present. In the Forest Temple Meetings, presided over by Mrs. A. G. Devereaux, Mrs. Susanne Harris gave some striking proofs of her mediumship. The amiability of the chairwoman contributes greatly to the success of these meetings, and so does that of Mr. John D. Lillie, chairman of the Auditorium gatherings, promoting good feeling all round.

There were also some mediums for materializations there, but when I saw at a seance with Mr. J. phantoms appear wearing paper crowns, and found that his cabinet had a double hinge, so that the door could be opened even when it was locked, I consider that such mediums can make no claim to confidence. I should recommend the directors not to allow any physical medium in the camp whom they had not previously tried under test conditions. The Theosophists would then have less foundations for many of their objections to Spiritualism. The late William Q. Judge, General Secretary of the American Section of the Theosophical Society, expressed some of these objections in his work, *The Ocean of Theosophy,* published by The Path, 144 Madison Avenue, New York, 1893, p. 149:

"I. At no time have these spirits given the laws governing any of the phenomena, except in a few instances, not accepted by the cult, where the Theosophical theory was advanced. As it would destroy such structures as those erected by A. J. Davis, these particular spirits fell into discredit.

"II. The spirits disagree among themselves, one stating the after-life to be very different from the description by another. These disagreements vary with the medium and the supposed theories of the deceased during life. One spirit admits reincarnation and others deny it.

"III. The spirits have discovered nothing in respect to history, anthropology, or other important matters, seeming to have less ability in that line than living men; and although they often claim to be men who lived in older civilisations, they show ignorance thereupon, or merely repeat recently published discoveries.

"IV. In these forty years no *rationale* of phenomena or of development of mediumship has been obtained from the spirits. Great philosophers are reported as speaking through mediums, but utter only drivel and merest commonplaces.

"V. The mediums come to physical and moral grief, are accused of fraud, are shown guilty of trickery, but the spirit guides and controls do not interfere to either prevent or save.

"VI. It is admitted that the guides and controls deceive and invite to fraud.

"VII. It is plainly to be seen through all that is reported of the spirits that their assertions and philosophy, if any, vary with the medium and the most advanced thought of living spiritualists. From all this and much more that could be adduced, the man of materialistic science is fortified in his ridicule, but the theosophist has to conclude that the entities, if there be any communicating, are not human spirits, and that the explanations are to be found in some other theories."

Mr. Judge says further:

"Materialisation of a form out of the air, independent of the medium's physical body, is a fact! Three explanations are offered: First, that the astral body of the living medium detaches itself from its corpus and assumes the appearance of the so-called spirit; for one of the properties of the astral matter is capacity to reflect an image existing unseen in ether. Second, the actual astral shell of the deceased—wholly devoid of his or her spirit and conscience—becomes visible and tangible when the condition of air and ether is such as to so alter the vibrations of the molecules of the astral shell that it may become visible. The phenomena of density and apparent weight are explained by other laws. Third, an unseen mass of electrical and magnetic matter is collected, and upon it is reflected out of the astral light a picture of any desired person either dead or living. This is taken to be the 'spirit' of such persons, but it is not, and has been justly called by H. P. Blavatsky, 'a psychological fraud,' because it pretends to be what it is not."

After the experiments of Professor Crookes with Florence Cook, those of Professor Richet and many others with Eusapia Paladino, after the experiences with Miller described in this book, and the extensive literature on materialisations by learned and accurate observers, there is only one answer to be given to the above three theosophical explanations of materialisations: He who can understand it, let him understand it; let him who is too stupid leave it alone.

Such are the principal objections raised by Theosophy against Spiritualism. I may spare myself the trouble of refuting them in detail by extracts from spiritualist authors, seeing that they have already been answered by Professor Brofferio and Privy Councillor Aksakof; the former has given a detailed reply to them. I grant that such objections may apply to a large number of mediums, but after eliminating cases of fraud and of animism, there remain facts upon which Aksakof has laid much emphasis, and which necessarily imply spirit action. In this respect my experience has been the same as his: "As years went by," he says, "the weak points of Spiritualism became more evident and more numerous. The insignificance of the communications, the poverty of their intellectual content, and finally the fraud, etc., in short, a host of doubts, objections, and aberrations of every kind, greatly increased the difficulties of the problem. Such impressions were well calculated to discourage one, if on the other hand we had not had at our disposal a series of indisputable facts."

Mr. Cromwell Varley, the well-known electrician, once asked the spirits why they had never revealed any new scientific knowledge. They replied, very plausibly, that for this purpose they would need a scientifically trained medium, capable of expressing scientific ideas intelligibly. Varley calculated that on an average there would only be a chance of obtaining a scientific medium once in ten generations.

I willingly recognize that Spiritualism has serious faults; more than once I have gone home from spiritualistic seances completely disheartened, like Hermann Handrich, who recently wrote: "I know of spirits who for some decades have made their bow before very mixed audiences of the curious two or three times, or even more, a week; these are spirit controls in evening dress, Indians in war-paint, uttering stereotyped phrases; others who pass to-day for such and such a sister, betrothed, wife, etc., and to-morrow for quite another. These are beings who must be regarded with suspicion, who lend themselves to feelings of every kind. It is certain that, under such conditions, intercourse between this world and the other is aimless and indeed not at all desirable. Total annihilation of individuality would be preferable to a life of vampirism and borrowed characters of this sort."

E. von Hartmann (*Die Geisterhypothese des Spiritismus,* Leipzig, 1891) says much the same thing. On the other hand, I have myself come into contact with spirits whose lofty expressions always impressed me. Moreover, we read in Mme. d'Espérance's book, *Shadowland,* that her spirit control, Humnor Stafford, talked with Englishmen of science on scientific questions, and taught them things that were new to them. This depends principally on the character of the medium and of the sitters. The law of attraction plays the principal part, even here, in great measure! So long as mediums were persecuted, like the late Valesca Töpfer and Anna Rothe, and almost all others in Europe, there is not much to be hoped for, seeing that sensitiveness cannot easily accommodate itself to the opposition of sceptics—scarcely to distrust, much less to violence—and without sensitiveness there can be no phenomena! Certainly the unlimited liberty which prevails in America has produced a crowd of fraudulent mediums who think of nothing but gaining money by their tricks.

Theosophy, moreover, only gives us inward "revelations," which may be of greater value, but may also be of less, than those of Spiritualism; there is no sense in speaking of the revelations of spiritualistic phenomena as being of less value than those of Theosophy. The difference between them is indisputable. *Experiment* alone can convince the world of individual survival; this is a view that du Prel communicated to me as his own, in a private letter, as far back as 1893.

On September 16th, 1907, the *Osservatore Romano*, the official organ of the Vatican, published an Encyclical on "Modernism in the Faith." It is really an elaboration of the syllabus published a few weeks before.

The encyclical sets forth that modernism is a serious danger to the Church, refers in detail to the various features of modernism and condemns it as dangerous in philosophy, faith, theology, history, criticism and reform, and arrives at the conclusion that modernism is a synthesis of all heresy and must logically lead to atheism.

The encyclical makes the following provisions:

First—The teaching of philosophy, positive theology, etc., is to be carried on in the Church schools and universities, but in a Catholic spirit.

Second—Modernists are to be removed from professorships and the direction of educational institutions.

Third—The clergy and faithful are not to be allowed to read modernist publications.

Fourth—A committee of censorship is to be established in every diocese to pass upon the publications which the clergy and faithful shall be permitted to read.

Fifth—The encyclical of the late Pope Leo XIII. prohibiting the clergy from assuming the direction of publications without their bishop's permission, and providing for supervision of the work of ecclesiastical writers, is confirmed.

Sixth—Ecclesiastical congresses, except on rare occasions, are prohibited.

Seventh—A council is to be constituted in every diocese to combat modern errors.

Books are not to be published without permission from the authorities. Similar enactments were issued by the Archbishop Berthold of Mainz in 1486, Pope Alexander VI. in 1501, and Leo X. in 1515. The Council of Trent not only ordered a strict censorship to be maintained, but also commanded that an Index should be published of books the reading of which was prohibited. This *Index Librorum prohibitorum* appeared in 1564 along with the *Decreta et Canones Concilii Tridentini,* and large numbers of works published since that time have been "placed on the Index." Smaller numbers of Kant's and Lessing's works have not

An Occultist's Travels. 243

been sold, because they were on the Index. Orthodoxy would now appear to be incompatible with free research, free exercise of thought. Not, indeed, universally incompatible, but only in those matters in which they might lead to conflict with the teachings of the Church; but, of course, theology is just one of those subjects. If a theologian wishes to investigate freely, he must leave the Catholic Church. An astronomer, a physicist, a zoologist, a biologist, an historian, so long as he confines himself strictly to the scientific aspect of his subject, has no need to leave it.

The naïve idea that there can be a man or a human authority which is armed by God with authority to decide with unfailing certainty between truth and error in matters of religion and ethics, and that the Bishop of Rome for the time being is that man, cannot be upheld in the present state of our historical and psychological knowledge.

Metapsychism (Spiritualism) and the employment of animal magnetism are unreservedly condemned by the Catholic Church.

"Viele Frösche bequaken den Fernhintreffer Apollo;

Doch der Gott schwebt leicht uber die Sümpfe
hinweg."* —*Platen.*

*Many frogs croak at Apollo darting down from afar; but the God sweeps easily over the marshes and away.

THE END.